STORY STAKES

Your #1 Writing Skills Strategy
to Produce a Page-Turner
that Transforms Readers
into Raving Fans
of Your Screenplay
or Novel

H. R. D'COSTA

scribemeetsworld.com
Storytelling, Simplified

Copyright 2014, 2015 H. R. D'Costa. All rights reserved.

First ebook edition published in 2014.

Print edition published in 2015.

Note: This paperback edition contains additional material not included in ebook editions released prior to August 2015.

Cover image is adapted from *Music fans* by Dan Markeye, which is licensed under CC BY 2.0: https://www.flickr.com/photos/knowledge-test/9900077524.

Print edition ISBN: 978-1-5153-1504-9

Printed in the United States of America

v 1.1

CONTENTS

Introduction 7

CHAPTER ONE

11 Types of Story Stakes Which Increase Tension and Reader Engagement 15

Stake Type #1: General Protection................... 16
Stake Type #2: Demise 18
Stake Type #3: Livelihood 20
Stake Type #4: Freedom 25
Stake Type #5: Reputation............................ 26
Stake Type #6: Sanity................................. 29
Stake Type #7: Access................................ 30
Stake Type #8: Regret 31
Stake Type #9: Suffering and Sacrifice............. 35
Stake Type #10: Justice 41
Stake Type #11: Hero Happiness 46
   Show Me the Money (and Something Else)!........... 49
Manufacturing a Mesmerizing MacGuffin 56

CHAPTER TWO

8 Modulating Factors Which Affect the Emotional Impact of the Stakes 63

Modulator #1: The Emotional Bond Between Audiences and the Hero 66
   Emotional Bond Wrecker #1: Too Much Delay 67
   Emotional Bond Wrecker #2: Potential Alienation 71
   Emotional Bond Wrecker #3: Dilution of Loyalty 74

Modulator #2: The Emotional Bond Between
Audiences and the Stakes............................78
    Forging the Audience-Stake Bond....................79
    6 Ways to Maintain the Audience-Stake Bond.........80
Modulator #3: Boundaries and Restrictions........89
    Time...90
    Resources..93
    Magical Powers.....................................94
Modulator #4: Vulnerable Populations...............96
Modulator #5: Hero Backstory.......................99
Modulator #6: Setting............................. 102
Modulator #7: Contingency Stakes.................. 103
Modulator #8: The Secret Modulator............... 105

CHAPTER THREE

The Story Stake Matrix: Groundwork................................. 107

The Hierarchy of Needs............................ 108
The Cost of Participation......................... 110
    High vs. Low Costs................................ 111
    Cost vs. Stakes...................................112
The 4 Cells of the Story Stake Matrix............. 118

CHAPTER FOUR

Cell #1: Low Cost, Spiritual Needs...... 123

Comedies, Romances,
and Romantic Comedies............................ 124
Action Movies, Thrillers, Mysteries, Dramas,
and Fantasy & Science-Fiction.................... 132
    Raising the Stakes and Shifting into Cell #2......... 135

CHAPTER FIVE
Cell #2: Low Cost, Safety Needs........ 141

Comedies and Romantic Comedies................ 142

A Special Note for Romance Novelists............ 143

How to Use Stakes to Enhance
the Initial Premise of Your Romance Novel 144

When Your Hero or Heroine
Must Make High-Cost Sacrifices 150

Action Movies, etc.. 153

CHAPTER SIX
Cell #3: High Cost, Safety Needs 169

Beginning Act 2A in Cell #3 170

9 Ways to Make Your High-Stake Climax
Even More of a Nail-Biter 173

Avoiding the Anticlimactic Ending................... 181

CHAPTER SEVEN
Cell #4: High Cost, Spiritual Needs...... 189

Selling Stakes of Justice 191

Selling Stakes of Reputation 197

Selling Stakes of Happiness......................... 201

CHAPTER EIGHT
The Story Stake Matrix: Wrapping Up...205

Final Pointers for Cells #1–#4 205

The Basic Story Stake Action Plan 207

Helpful Resources for You........................... 209

Free Story Stake Worksheet 209

3 Story Stake Exercises 210

CHAPTER NINE
5 Additional Purposes for Story Stakes 213

Craft a Dynamic Opening 214
Humanize Antagonists 218
Enhance Pacing 221
Create Suspects and Red Herrings 222
Advance the Plot Without
Sacrificing Your Characters 224

CHAPTER TEN
Making Real Magic 229

INTRODUCTION

YOU'RE A WRITER. YOU KNOW THE DREAM. IT GOES something like this:

Sell your screenplay for six figures or write a best-selling novel…

…tell your boss, "From now on, you can get your own coffee…"

…take a much-deserved vacation, to Paris, or perhaps to Hawaii…

…and when you finally return home, make a living through your writing.

Lost in these fantasies, it's easy to lose sight of a basic truth: **it all starts with one reader**.

How does that big spec sale happen? How does a novel enjoy massive sales?

First, someone becomes so captivated by your story, he can't put it down. He keeps turning the pages, faster and faster, till he's reached the very end.

Second, once this reader has finished reading your screenplay or novel, he doesn't promptly reach for the next story in his stack of unread scripts or novels.

Nope.

Before beginning his next reading adventure, he passionately recommends your story to everyone he knows.

His boss, his colleagues, his friends, his niece, his grandma—to all of them—his message is the same:

"Read this screenplay. Watch this movie. Buy this book."

So, how do you begin this process?

How do you capture the attention of one reader, the reader whose positive recommendation could change your life?

You might think that readers will keep on turning the pages of your story because they like your protagonist, or think that he's cool.

But that's a mistake.

Readers aren't going to spend hours with James Bond while he sips one of his signature martinis just because he's a badass.

They're not going to hang out with Jerry Maguire while he feeds his goldfish just because he's found his conscience.

They're not going to stick around with Erin Brockovich while she gets a manicure just because she's funny and feisty.

I know, I know. These scenarios are boring. I made them that way to drive home my point.

Even if you jazz up these scenes with more exciting genre elements—thrills, action, romance, humor, or drama—that's still not enough to keep audiences interested for the long haul.

Audiences need something more than just fun. They need something more than just entertainment.

They need a reason to care about what happens in your story.

This is where story stakes come in.

Because of stakes, your hero can't walk away from his problem. As a result, readers won't be able to walk away from your story.

See, stakes make readers wonder if your protagonist will succeed or fail at his goal.

It's a whole new ball game.

Now, your readers will *worry* about him. Now, they're under *tension*.

Finishing your script or novel is no longer optional.

It's mandatory.

That's because the ONLY way for readers to relieve this tension is to keep turning the pages of your story till they reach its end.

They can't check their voicemail or wash their dishes or fold their laundry or even go to sleep.

They *must* keep reading (or watching).

They need to discover how Bond saves the world, how Jerry wins the girl, and if Erin can bring justice to a small town.

To put it another way, likeability (or coolness, etc.)—even a high-concept premise—may get your readers in the door, *but stakes are why they stay for supper.*

Even if you've included nail-biting stakes in your story, you're not home free yet. That's only the first step. You've still got to get readers raving about your screenplay or novel.

To do this, you need to understand one simple little thing: **readers become passionate about the stories that give them the most intense emotional experience**.

Look at *Taken*, for instance. Kidnapping plots are hardly unique. Yet, this film blew away the competition and became a blockbuster success.

How?

The filmmakers took the basic premise, which was emotionally charged to begin with, and amplified its intensity. They made audiences root even *harder* for the hero's success.

At first, this may seem impossible. Bryan is trying to rescue his daughter from a prostitution ring—a serious situation. How can audiences become even *more* invested in its outcome?

Through skillful manipulation of the story stakes, that's how.

If you know how to use stakes wisely, you can easily craft stories that bring readers to the emotional edge—and thus stand out in a crowded marketplace.

Master story stakes, and you can eclipse the competition. This writing guide will show you how.

Specifically, we'll cover:

11 Types of Story Stakes Which Increase Tension and Reader Engagement

Some of them you already know. A few will be new. At the very least, you'll have a convenient list to check the next time you need a new reason for your hero to save the day, trick your leading lady, or chase down a suspect.

Plus, we'll cover best practices. That way, you'll get the most mileage out of the stakes you choose to include in your story.

8 Modulating Factors Which Affect the Emotional Impact of the Stakes

Think of modulating factors like the audio control knobs on a stereo system. They can either turn up the emotional "volume," or…they can mute it.

In other words, through modulating factors, audiences will feel more (or less) intensely about *the same set of story stakes*.

Oftentimes, modulating factors are the secret to wringing out the extra drop of emotion that will give your story an advantage over others in its genre.

The Story Stake Matrix

This is where we put everything together. It's a tool that will show you:

- how to use stakes to craft a premise with more commercial appeal
- **how to raise the stakes (even when they're already high)**
- how to avoid an anticlimactic ending

Let's focus on that second benefit for a minute.

Several writing guides will tell you that to keep readers glued to the pages of your story, you've got to raise the stakes. But, these books are frustratingly vague on how to accomplish this career-making task.

This book is not vague. This book will give you specific strategies you can use right away to make high stakes feel *even higher*.

Sounds good, right?

But before we continue, you should be aware of the following:

(1) Unless otherwise indicated, the tips in this book apply equally to screenplays and novels.

Despite this, I primarily use film examples to illustrate my points. That's because movies are more universal.

Chances are greater that you've watched, rather than read, *The Silence of the Lambs*.

Even if you're a romance buff, it's more likely you've rented *The Proposal* than skimmed a novel entitled *Andrew and Margaret's Fake Engagement*.

On paper, the titles of films adapted from novels (or a TV series) appear the same as novel (or TV) titles. Customarily, all are indicated via italics. But since I mainly rely on film examples, unless otherwise noted, it's safe to assume I'm referencing the film version only.

If you're interested in writing TV procedurals, the tips in this book can help you write a stronger spec script. But with rare exception, none of the illustrative examples come from television shows. You'll have to use your own judgment to determine how to adapt these tips and make them work for your situation.

(2) I've done my best to pull examples from a variety of genres. But, I'll admit, there is a slant toward stories that include action, mystery, and thrills (including hybrids like action comedies, sci-fi thrillers, and romantic suspense).

That being said, I've included several examples from comedies and romantic comedies. Additionally, there is a special section with tips just for romance novelists.

Oh, of course, using lots of examples means there are some spoilers too.

(3) This guide focuses on (a) the stakes associated with your protagonist's overall goal, and (b) how to use them to increase tension and emotion in your story.

However, stakes can be used for other purposes. I'll discuss five of them in a special chapter at the end of this book.

(4) I analyze movies using three-act structure. You might not like using three-act structure. That's cool. You can still benefit from this writing guide.

Where appropriate, just replace Act One with "the beginning," Act Two with "the middle," and Act Three with "the end" of your story. That way, you'll be able to make use of all the tips in this book without any quibbling over structure.

(5) I'm an outliner, or "a plotter." Personally, I think it's going to be a lot easier to incorporate a particular modulating factor, for instance, when your story's in outline form.

Even so, if you're someone who writes on the fly, without an outline, a.k.a. "a pantser," you can still get mileage out of this book. Instead of incorporating the tips discussed herein into your outline, you'll use them to evaluate your rough draft and to determine what kind of changes you might want to make.

(6) Finally, for the sake of simplicity, I tend to stick to masculine nouns and pronouns.

Okay, that's all.

To take another step toward enthralled readers, raving fans…and blockbuster success, continue reading!

- chapter one -

11 TYPES OF STORY STAKES WHICH INCREASE TENSION AND READER ENGAGEMENT

Simply put, stakes are the negative consequences of failure.

If your protagonist fails to achieve his goal, bad things will happen.

Very bad things.

(Of course, the definition of *bad* varies across genres.)

Specifically, stakes are the reason why your hero *cannot* walk away from dangerous or unpleasant tasks.

In action movies, the price of failure is often death; in romances, it's a broken heart.

While loss of life and loss of happiness are commonly used as story stakes, there are, as you'll discover, plenty of others. For your convenience, here is a list of the 11 major types of story stakes we'll discuss in this chapter:

- general protection
- demise
- livelihood
- freedom
- reputation
- sanity
- access
- regret
- suffering and sacrifice
- justice
- hero happiness

For a deeper exploration of each, keep reading!

Stake Type #1: General Protection

Typically found in action movies, thrillers, and fantasy & science-fiction, general stakes involve the fate of a collective group residing in a particular location:

- a bus (*Speed*)
- a post-apocalyptic city (*Divergent*)
- a fairy tale kingdom (*Snow White & the Huntsman*)
- a nation (*Braveheart*)
- a continent (*Sherlock Holmes: A Game of Shadows*)

- an empire (*Gladiator*)
- a planet (*Star Trek* (2009))
- an entire galaxy (*Star Wars*)

If the hero fails in his quest, this location and all of its inhabitants may be completely destroyed. Alternately, this location may still exist, but its citizens will be governed by gross tyranny (which, I'd argue, is an even worse fate).

Whatever the consequence, stakes of general protection focus on how the hero's failure will affect others, not on how it will affect him personally.

Sometimes, stakes of protection revolve around a specific individual rather than the population of a certain place.

This usually happens when the protagonist's profession requires him to keep others safe. If he fails in his duties, then innocent or powerful people will die or suffer great harm.

For instance, the protagonist could be:

- an FBI agent trying to save a bunch of beauty pageant contestants (*Miss Congeniality*)
- a Secret Service agent trying to save the president (*In the Line of Fire*)
- a DEA agent trying to protect an important witness (*Traffic*)
- a US Navy lawyer trying to acquit two marines accused of murder (*A Few Good Men*)
- a forensic psychologist trying to rescue a kidnapped girl (*Along Came a Spider*)

While stakes of general protection form the cornerstone of many action movies and thrillers, so does our next type of story stake…

Stake Type #2: Demise

When these stakes are in play, the penalty is death. However, unlike stakes of general protection, these stakes emphasize what the hero will *personally* lose.

If he fails at the climax, someone precious to him will die.

In a medical thriller, this loved one may contract the deadly virus that threatens the whole nation. In a horror film or paranormal romance, this person might experience a metaphorical death and lose his or her soul.

But, on the whole, if stakes of demise are in play, the means are usually not that creative. The villain simply plans to kill this person outright.

For instance, in *Die Hard*, the general stakes consist of the Nakatomi Plaza employees Hans Gruber has taken hostage. Unfortunately for hero John McClane, one of these hostages is his estranged wife.

The threat to her life comprises the stakes of demise. If McClane doesn't thwart Gruber, it will be game over for the hostages *and* Mrs. McClane (or Ms. Gennaro if you prefer).

Writers sometimes complain that the hero's loved one always gets taken hostage by the end of a movie. They resolutely vow not to fall prey to this cliché.

But it's commonplace for a reason.

Returning to the Die Hard franchise helps explain why. In the DVD commentary for *Live Free or Die Hard*, director Len Wiseman discusses why he wanted to change the script so that McClane would have to save his daughter Lucy:

> At the end of the day, somebody who's out to save the United States…you know, a pretty bold mission, I think people can't connect so much with a larger idea like that, and if there's something emotional, some kind of personal hook, I thought the people would connect to it better.

Later on, actor Bruce Willis will equate Lucy's kidnapping scene to the classic movie staple of tying the female heroine to the railroad tracks. In response, Wiseman adds:

> The whole motivation for McClane, even if he had this mission of saving the United States and the whole infrastructure is going to be taken down, and he's got to save that…people can't connect so much with that…people don't personally respond to that, but you can understand losing or trying to get to someone you care about.

And if those observations don't convince you, listen to the director's DVD commentary for *Die Hard 2*. Renny Harlin expresses the exact same sentiment!

So you see, John McClane doesn't consistently suffer stakes of demise because the filmmakers run out of creativity during each movie's production. He's the unluckiest cop in America because his personal tragedies make his experiences more accessible, and consequently, elicit the *strongest* emotional response from audiences.

This raises an interesting point: are general stakes necessary at all? Can audiences enjoy a film (or novel) where there are no general stakes, no larger mission?

The heroes of *Taken*, the first *Red* film, and the Bourne franchise are all CIA-trained operatives, but none of them are, as is typically the case, trying to save the world…just their own skin.

Since these films were massive hits, the answer seems to be a resounding yes. Emulating this strategy could be just the ticket to putting a fresh spin on your next thriller!

So far, in this discussion of stakes of demise, we've mainly focused on the death of someone precious to the hero.

What about the hero himself?

If he's about to die by the villain's hand, isn't his life at stake too?

The answer to that question, unfortunately, isn't entirely straightforward. We'll return to it later on, when we discuss the story stake matrix.

Stake Type #3: Livelihood

With stakes of livelihood, if the protagonist doesn't achieve his goal, then he (or someone precious to him) will lose gainful employment.

If this setback only signifies that the protagonist will have to stop indulging in his gourmet cheese addiction, these stakes will have no bite.

Losing his job should jeopardize his own survival or his ability to support people he loves—a spouse, siblings, children, etc.

These stakes are especially effective when combined with any of the following:

- The protagonist has invested significant resources to achieve his current position.
- The protagonist had to fight against parental disapproval or societal constraints to get where he is.
- The position itself is rare and difficult to obtain.
- The position is inextricably connected to the protagonist's self-esteem.
- The protagonist is unlikely to find future employment elsewhere.

To illustrate, let's examine *Night at the Museum*. Larry's been hired as the evening watchman at the Museum of Natural History. Unbeknownst to him, after the sun sets, the museum exhibits come to life. He must handle the ensuing chaos without losing his mind—or his life.

Now, I don't know about your taste in movies. You may think *Night* is an idiotic film. (I, for one, was annoyed by the extended antics with the monkey, although, as a whole, I think the movie provides decent family entertainment.)

But, I think we can both agree that it's a high-concept premise, the kind that makes a studio executive's eyes light up with dollar signs.

So, let's say you had developed a saleable concept like that. And you were having a blast coming up with lots of hilarious ways for the museum exhibits to wreak havoc for Larry.

Like the stunt in the movie with Rexy, the dinosaur skeleton who likes to play fetch with a giant bone, as if he were a cuddly puppy and not a carnivorous reptile. In a nice touch, the bone, by the way, is taken from Rexy's own body!

As fans of Blake Snyder's screenwriting guide *Save the Cat* might say, you nailed the "fun and games." You've come up with good stuff. But, it's not enough.

Here's why: Larry doesn't have to grapple with the unruly museum exhibits. He could just quit and avoid this headache altogether.

Problem solved…

…plot over…

…no more fun and games.

Enter stakes of livelihood.

To keep the plot going, while maintaining both credibility and comic mayhem, the story gives audiences several reasons why Larry can't leave his traumatic job. For one thing, he's in poor financial straits. He needs the money to pay his rent (and remove the boot from his car).

With his spotty job history, he's unlikely to find another position elsewhere. (Actually, it was a trial for him to even land the watchman job in the first place.)

We're not done yet. There's still one more issue to address. Larry's the kind of guy who avoids adversity rather than trying to overcome it.

This personality defect gives Larry the opportunity for character growth. But, it also means that even with his financial problems, he will be tempted to give up and quit.

In fact, at one point in the movie, he does!

The filmmakers could've changed Larry's personality, which would have ironed out this wrinkle, but that would've effectively wrecked Larry's character arc, and possibly, still strained credibility. Instead, to keep Larry motivated, the filmmakers deepened the stakes, connecting Larry's job to his relationship with his son, Nicky.

At the film's beginning, Larry feels emasculated because his ex-wife's new boyfriend is able to provide Nicky and her with the luxurious lifestyle Larry cannot. Even worse, Larry's ex-wife is worried about Larry's lack of stability.

If Larry doesn't get his life together, she will minimize his contact with Nicky. (Technically, this threat brings another kind of stake into the picture. We'll go into more particulars when we reach stake type #7.)

Later, the story will zoom in on the way Nicky perceives his dad. Larry's ex-wife fears that Nicky won't be able to handle being disappointed by his dad again. Her fears are not unjustified. Nicky, too, is starting to entertain doubts about his dad's ability to hold down a job and fulfill his promises.

To Larry, this is worst of all. To avoid having his son think he is a loser, Larry must keep his hellacious job as the night watchman.

These are great stakes.

They make it easy to buy into the idea that Larry will do whatever it takes to keep his job, tame the unruly museum exhibits, and impress his son. It's something that audiences can understand, relate to, and most important, root for.

To put it another way, the stakes give audiences a reason to care about what happens, to fully and wholeheartedly invest in Larry's comedic adventures.

Can you see how stakes, when well applied, can enhance the overall quality of your own story?

In this example, the stakes keep the plot going, enable Larry to have a meaningful character arc, *and* fuel the emotional core at the heart of the comedy. If you, like the filmmaking team behind *Night at the Museum*, harness the power of stakes, your story could enjoy similar blockbuster success.

Note: Although they both involve employment, stakes of livelihood do not encompass failure to get a promotion. That's because the losses they incur are not equivalent.

In the former, failure means the protagonist will be divested of all means of survival.

In the case of the latter, if he fails, the protagonist might be unhappy and dissatisfied. Nevertheless, he will still have his original position and the income it provides.

Hence, pursuit of a promotion is categorized by another stake type: hero happiness. We'll explore these stakes in more depth at the end of this chapter.

Stake Type #4: Freedom

When these stakes are in play, if the hero fails to achieve his goal, he (or someone precious to him) will lose his freedom, often through some system of confinement.

At first, you might think that the threat of incarceration is limited to thrillers and dramas. However, these stakes can be found in a variety of genres.

By the end of both workplace comedies *9 to 5* and *Horrible Bosses*, the protagonists must outwit their employers not just to keep their jobs but also to avoid lengthy jail sentences.

And in the fantasy *Harry Potter and the Chamber of Secrets*, Harry must confront the villain (and the villain's basilisk) in order to preserve the freedom of his friend, Hagrid, who is about to be sent to Azkaban, a prison for Great Britain's magical community. (That's one reason, at any rate.)

While these examples focus on jail, confinement certainly isn't limited to a prison cell. Characters who are trapped in a particular time (*Back to the Future*), place (*The Truman Show*), or time *and* place (*Groundhog Day*) also lack freedom. The outcome of the climax will determine whether these protagonists will regain their personal liberty.

In addition to geography and time, forms of entrapment can also encompass states of being and circumstance. For instance, in *Avatar*, Jake Sully's spinal injuries keep him confined to a wheelchair. The title of *Pirates of the Caribbean: The Curse of the Black Pearl* says it all: the pirates are trapped by a curse.

In mysteries, suspects may be driven to murder because they've become entrapped by blackmail. In domestic dramas, the heroine (or hero) could be trapped in an emotionally controlling relationship.

In thrillers, an antagonist, driven by the desire to kill or capture the hero, may relentlessly pursue him. No matter the slant put upon the antagonist's intentions, the outcome is the same: the hero will not enjoy true freedom until the final confrontation with his pursuer—assuming a happy ending—liberates the hero for good.

Stake Type #5: Reputation

Here's an admonition, commonly attributed to Socrates, which you may've come across before:

> **Regard your good name as the richest jewel you can possibly be possessed of—for credit is like fire; when once you have kindled it, you may easily preserve it, but if you once extinguish it, you will find it an arduous task to rekindle it again.**

In light of this comparison, it's easy to see why stakes of reputation—whether they involve someone's good name, legacy, or honor—incite protagonists to take action.

Practically speaking, the protagonist's reputation will typically be under siege at the outset of the story. Alternatively, the protagonist may begin in possession of a glowing reputation, but the choices he (or the antagonist) makes during the protagonist's journey bring it into disrepute.

Either way, the outcome of the climax will either restore the protagonist's reputation or mar it forever.

Stakes of reputation are especially effective when tied to other stakes, like livelihood or freedom. For example, if a hero is framed for a crime he didn't commit, he must clear his name to preserve both his reputation and his freedom.

The Fugitive and *Mission: Impossible IV* are examples of this model. The latter, however, differs significantly from the former in one key respect. In *The Fugitive*, only Richard Kimble's fate hangs in the balance. In *Mission IV*, Ethan Hunt must reclaim his reputation while, simultaneously, saving general stakes from disaster.

That's just one variation. There are plenty more. Your protagonist doesn't have to be framed in order for stakes of reputation to have emotional weight.

Look at historical novels. A heroine will often have to zealously guard her reputation—or face grave consequences. Since most methods of employment would be prohibited to her, unless she were independently wealthy, marriage would likely be her only hope of survival. A good reputation could help her secure an advantageous marriage, and thus ensure her future. A scandalous reputation could ruin those prospects entirely.

No murder, no world-saving mission. Yet, in this context, these stakes are very much a matter of life and death.

So far, we've focused on how stakes of reputation affect a protagonist's immediate situation. But, perhaps, your hero is not just worried about his current state of affairs. Perhaps, he's also concerned about the legacy he leaves behind.

Take *Iron Man*. Regretting that he's built his fortune by profiting from war, Tony vows that Stark Industries will reverse course and cease manufacturing weapons. With this decision, Tony can rest easy that his legacy won't be one of death and destruction.

Obadiah Stane has other ideas in mind. He intends to kill Tony and take over Stark Industries. That would be bad enough on its own, but that's not all Obadiah wants.

In addition, Obadiah plans to apply life-saving technology, which Tony has developed and hopes to use for good, to manufacture more powerful weapons. This would ruin Tony's legacy—making Tony's dire predicament even worse.

Stakes pertaining to reputation are often overlooked by beginners who gravitate toward stakes that are literally a matter of life and death. Although, on the surface, stakes of reputation may not seem that exciting, don't underestimate their power.

They can add extra richness and nuance to the standard action plot, elevating your story above the competition. Not only that, they have tremendous ability to elicit an even deeper degree of emotional investment from audiences.

In fact, they are a great way to raise the stakes, when the stakes are already high to begin with. We'll discuss this idea in greater detail when we explore the story stake matrix.

Stake Type #6: Sanity

These stakes are in play when failure will trigger an alteration to the consciousness of the protagonist (or someone he loves).

These individuals may lose their minds. Their memories may be tampered with. In their most egregious manifestation, these stakes are merged with stakes of freedom to produce mind control. If the hero fails, then he (and likely other characters), will have their minds controlled and manipulated by the antagonist.

Although stakes of sanity are not often used, when they are put into play, they can be quite chilling and effective. In *Minority Report*, for example, the threat of confinement (stakes of freedom) feels even more horrifying because it is accompanied by a tampering of the prisoner's consciousness.

We didn't really cover this earlier on, but the loss of sanity can be paired with stakes of general protection to provide a unique, albeit perverse, twist on the standard "save the world" plot.

In *Batman Begins*, the villain doesn't intend to kill the citizens of Gotham outright. Instead, by distilling the hallucinogenic properties of a rare blue flower and polluting their drinking water with it, he plans to drive them all insane with fear.

He can then take a step back and sadistically watch from the sidelines as Gotham's finest turn against each other and destroy their city themselves.

Stake Type #7: Access

When these stakes are invoked, the protagonist will lose access to someone meaningful to him, or in some cases, an entire community (as in the Amish practice of shunning, for example).

In perhaps their most poignant manifestation, these story stakes involve the relationship between parent and child. If the protagonist fails to achieve his goal, then he will lose contact with his children. Indeed, custody battles are fertile grounds for both conflict and story stakes.

These stakes can elicit a strong emotional response whether the parent has always realized the worth of his children (as in *Mrs. Doubtfire*), or has, through the course of his journey, come to that realization (as in *Liar Liar*).

The emotional core of *Inception* also revolves around stakes of access. Unlike the above examples, there's a slightly different emphasis. If Dom Cobb fails, he will not lose access to his children, but rather, his chance to regain it.

In all three of these films, regardless of the hero's success, the children's health and safety are assured. If that is not the case (as in the drug-addict-daughter plot thread in *Traffic*), then stakes of demise are in play, not stakes of access.

Sometimes, the focus of these stakes isn't on access to a person, but on access to a specific place—oftentimes a home. Whether these lodgings consist of a medieval European castle, a log cabin on the Western frontier, or a standard subdivision clone, the threat of losing home ownership contains great emotional power.

As a variation of this idea, examine the second Harry Potter film. In it, Harry must discover (and subdue) whatever's lurking around in *The Chamber of Secrets*.

If he doesn't, not only will Hagrid go to prison, but Hogwarts will also close. Since the school of witchcraft and wizardry provides Harry with nurturing and affection which is absent from his home life, this loss is significant. As such, it adds even more emotional resonance to the other stakes already in play.

Stake Type #8: Regret

Stakes of regret typically manifest in one of two ways. The first is what I like to call the "missed opportunity" variation.

In it, the protagonist entertains some kind of dream. Furthermore, it's usually something that he could've easily accomplished if he had put his mind to it.

Unfortunately, due to fear, misplaced priorities, or some other reason, he didn't act soon enough. Now, the inciting incident has turned his world topsy-turvy, precluding him from acting on this desire at all.

Consequently, failure at the climax doesn't just mean that the protagonist will fail to accomplish the overall goal driving the main plot. Failure will also trigger the sting of regret.

Success, too, contains double meaning. If the hero wins, it doesn't just mean that he will save the day.

It gives him a second chance.

It reopens a window of opportunity that would've been permanently closed to him had he failed in his mission.

For instance, because of setup established at the beginnings of *Collateral*, *The Fellowship of the Ring*, and *Taken*, audiences know that Max wants to start his own limo service, Sam wants to ask Rosie Cotton to dance, and Bryan wants to make up for past parental neglect, respectively.

Actually, to Bryan's credit, he was in the midst of trying to make amends to his daughter, but was interrupted midway. Nevertheless, he shares the same fate as the other protagonists listed above. Should they fail in their overall missions, they will never regain the opportunity to realize their secondary desires.

As a practical note, it's not mandatory for audiences to witness your hero achieving this secondary desire by the end of your story. In *Collateral*, audiences don't see Max launch his own business; it's enough for them to know that he can, having bested the villain, avail himself of this opportunity.

All the same, the achievement of your hero's secondary desire will likely yield potent fodder for the resolution of your screenplay or novel—as is the case in both *Taken* and *Fellowship*. (Although, in the latter, it should be noted, this resolution won't be depicted until *The Return of the King*.)

In the second common manifestation of stakes of regret, emphasis is placed on redemption rather than missed opportunity.

The hero had an opportunity in the past—took it—and failed. Ever since, he's been plagued by regret or guilt.

Flash-forward to the present.

The hero is given a goal which, in some way, echoes the goal he failed to achieve before. This is his chance to redeem himself—and he knows it.

If he succeeds now, he will not only save the day in the present, he will also be relieved of the regret haunting him from the past.

The Silence of the Lambs utilizes this technique with great sophistication. Orphaned, Clarice Starling was sent to live with distant relatives on a Montana ranch. One morning, she woke up to a strange sound, the sound of lambs screaming. She tried to free the animals, but they wouldn't leave their pens.

Because they wouldn't leave, she did. Carrying one lamb with her, Clarice ran away as fast as she could. She didn't get far. When she was brought back to the ranch, the rancher was so mad by what she had done, he sent her to a Lutheran orphanage.

He also killed the lamb she had tried to rescue. To this day, she still wakes up, terrorized by the sound of lambs screaming.

Now a promising FBI agent, Clarice has come a long way since then. Even so, her guilt over her inability to have rescued even one little lamb continues to plague her.

If, in the present, she can save a young woman from a serial killer, it will redeem Clarice for her past failure. Alleviated of guilt, perhaps Clarice will no longer be haunted by the cries of the lambs.

In all of the examples above, you'll notice that there are greater stakes in play than stakes of regret. (As a matter of fact, stakes of regret can never stand alone. They must be connected to another type of story stake.)

In *Collateral*, if Max doesn't follow Vincent's instructions, Max might be the hit man's next target. In the *Lord of the Rings* trilogy, if Sam doesn't help Frodo destroy the ring of power, all of Middle-earth could perish.

In *Taken*, if Bryan doesn't find his daughter, she could be raped or even killed. In *Silence*, if Clarice doesn't find the serial killer in time, he will claim yet another victim.

In the context of these stakes, do audiences even care about the protagonists' personal demons?

Yes, actually, they do.

Few (if any) readers have experience with hit men or prostitution rings or serial killers. None, I'd wager, have ever gone toe-to-toe against a malicious eye of flame.

Regret, on the other hand, is something audiences can instantly relate to. They've made regret's acquaintance; they have felt his bitter sting. They know him far more intimately than they could ever come to know Middle-earth.

This familiarity deepens their identification even further, giving them a more poignant experience—and gaining you a more powerful story.

There's another benefit at work, too. Overcoming regret isn't as exciting as, let's say, flying. Yet, for many, it is equally as impossible. When heroes get to say good-bye to their regret, audiences can vicariously partake in this experience.

Their own emotional burdens lighten, if only just a little. As a storyteller, this is, perhaps, one of the greatest gifts you can bestow on the world.

Stake Type #9: Suffering and Sacrifice

Like stakes of regret, there's an element of contingency embodied within stakes of suffering and sacrifice. If the hero wins, he will save the girl, save the world, save the day.

Meaningful in its own right, sure, but in this case, it has additional significance: *it means that his suffering was worthwhile, that his sacrifices were not made in vain.*

Consider the alternative, and you'll see how powerful these stakes can be. If the hero fails, it means that all the pain he has endured, all the sacrifices he has made…were pointless. A terrifying thought, and one whose universality gives these stakes an added edge.

Now that we've examined stakes of suffering and sacrifice in tandem, let's look at them individually.

Stakes of Suffering

Without hardship, there's little conflict in your story, and you're stripping it of any entertainment value. That's one reason to give your hero several obstacles to overcome throughout the middle of your story. Stakes of suffering provide another.

Each time your hero overcomes an ordeal, you add more suffering to his balance sheet. The price of defeat becomes higher.

Failure doesn't just mean that Frank will lose a prestigious horse race (*Seabiscuit*), that Greg won't get engaged (*Meet the Parents*), or that Riggs and Murtaugh won't nab the bad guys (*Lethal Weapon 2*).

Failure also means that Frank (and Seabiscuit) underwent painful rehabilitation, that Greg took a humiliating lie detector test, and that Murtaugh spent all night sitting on a toilet with a bomb rigged to it…

…in vain.

In other words, through stakes of suffering, audiences become even more emotionally invested in the outcome of the climax because its consequences have grown in meaning.

Conversely, audiences can become rather apathetic toward the climax because the hero hasn't suffered at all.

Thus, to a certain degree, every story makes use of these stakes. Well, I should amend that. Every *well-crafted* story incorporates stakes of suffering by putting the hero through a variety of ordeals during Act Two.

Even if you're sure that you've put your protagonist through his paces throughout your story, be on the lookout for ways to add to your protagonist's balance sheet of suffering.

Interestingly, in an early draft of *As Good As It Gets* (written by Mark Andrus and dated May 1992), Melvin Udall easily procures a physician to check up on Carol's sick son at her apartment. House calls are pricey, but money's not a problem for Melvin.

In the final film version however, Melvin endures greater suffering than a blow to his bank account. The physician is no mere random medical professional; he's the husband of Melvin's publisher. And Melvin has to grovel to get her to even ask her husband to perform this favor.

Melvin's prostration is especially noteworthy because Melvin hates to yield the upper hand. Despite his aversion, he humbles himself anyway. Hence, audiences become more invested in his quest to win over Carol (even when, shortly thereafter, his bout of groveling is followed by his typical rudeness).

Technically, you could say that in this example, Melvin's suffering embodies a specific kind of ordeal: the sacrifice of his pride. Which brings us to…

Stakes of Sacrifice

Stakes of sacrifice are exactly what they sound like. A key character has to give up something of value, usually for the greater good. This character, in essence, may choose to place precedence on one stake over another (often his own chances of happiness; see stake type #11).

Since they involve a specific kind of ordeal, stakes of sacrifice are not used as extensively as stakes of suffering.

Typically:

- The hero must give up something in order to embark on his journey and pursue his Act Two goal.
- The hero is offered a way out, but refuses, in order to save others.
- The hero must sacrifice something precious to him in order to forge ahead.
- Someone precious to the hero makes a sacrifice (often of his or her own life or happiness) so the hero can advance toward the climax.

The Return of the King provides us with an interesting variation to study. To save Middle-earth, Aragorn does everything he can to help Frodo destroy the ring of power. But the stakes for Aragorn run more personal than that.

If he fails, his love interest, Arwen, will die. That would be bad enough. The story manages the near-impossible and makes this dire situation feel even worse.

How?

Through the power of sacrifice.

As an elf, Arwen had the chance to leave Middle-earth and enjoy a peaceful, immortal life elsewhere. Having faith in Aragorn, she forsakes this opportunity. If Aragorn (and Frodo) fail, her sacrifice will have been made in vain.

Because she had a way out—and didn't take it—her potential death is even more poignant than if she were an average Middle-earth maiden, who, although equally doomed, would not be in a position to make such a sacrifice in the first place.

When martyrdom entails death, sacrifice is fairly easy to conceptualize. If you're writing the type of story where your hero can't give up his own life, it becomes trickier to devise sacrifices that carry emotional weight. But it's not impossible.

Look at *Erin Brockovich*. Erin and Ed must take PG&E to court to make the utility company pay for its crimes. In a bold move which paid off, screenwriter Susannah Grant and director Steven Soderbergh chose to downplay the courtroom drama and focus on other elements of the story—especially the personal sacrifices Erin makes along the way.

For instance, in one scene, Erin's boyfriend tells her, on the phone, that her youngest daughter said her first word that day:

> **We had a pretty big event around here…Beth…started talking. We're all sitting around at lunch, and she pointed at a ball and said, "ball." Out of the blue like that. It was pretty intense, seeing somebody's first word.**

Recognizing what she's lost, in response, Erin cries.

She knows that if she hadn't been working on the PG&E case, then she probably would have been at home to hear that precious word. Her dedication to the case—to justice—cost her one of the greatest joys of parenthood.

Notice that this scene, while heartbreaking, does nothing to advance the plot. It's not needed to show how Erin eventually achieves victory. Although it slows down the momentum of the story, its inclusion is extremely beneficial. By learning about one of the prices Erin pays to continue her journey, audiences are likely to be even more invested in its outcome than they were originally.

In romances, the sacrifices made by the hero or heroine tend to follow certain patterns. In order to secure love (and, hence, happiness), the hero or heroine must sacrifice the protective mechanisms they've used to keep others at bay, and correspondingly, stave off the pain of rejection.

This is true of every reluctant protagonist in a romance. Depending on your plot, this protective mechanism may take on a specialized external form. It could be:

- false pretenses or a disguise
- a relationship that enables the protagonist to remain emotionally shallow (think of *Jerry Maguire*'s relationship with Avery)
- preoccupation with his or her career or professional advancement

Whatever the external form may be, the hero or heroine will have to shed—or sacrifice—it in order to achieve their goal of true love.

As a romantic comedy, *The Proposal* follows tradition to a T, but goes even one better, using stakes of sacrifice to overcome a major credibility hurdle. To keep her job, Margaret desperately needs Andrew to pretend to be her fiancé, a pretense that could send them both to jail. Plus, Andrew doesn't like Margaret all that much (not yet, anyway).

Andrew, quite logically, balks at the plan to shackle himself to his demanding boss. But Margaret browbeats him into compliance—quite believably—by reminding him of all the sacrifices he has already made to get where he is:

> **Bob is gonna fire you the second I'm gone. Guaranteed. That means you're out on the street alone looking for a job. That means all the time that we spent together, all the lattes, all the canceled dates, all the midnight Tampax runs, were all for nothing, and all your dreams of being an editor are gone.**

In other words, if Andrew refuses to go along with Margaret's scheme, all of his sacrifices (including those embarrassing tampon purchases!) will've been made in vain, and all his chances of advancement will evaporate. Understandably, the threat of these possibilities is terrifying enough to secure Andrew's cooperation, reluctance notwithstanding.

Having silenced credibility monitors, which could have raised a ruckus over Andrew's acquiescence, the story can merrily proceed toward its inevitable happy ending.

Stake Type #10: Justice

Once they understand the basic premise of your story, most (if not all) audience members will have a general wish to see the bad guy defeated. Stakes of justice invoke a more intense feeling than this basic yearning.

To put them into play, the antagonist must commit a truly heinous crime, either against the hero or another character. Audiences' desire to see the antagonist punished—and justice served—fuels their emotional involvement in the climax.

The way they see it, if the bad guys go down, then a fundamental wrong will, to a certain degree, be redressed. But if the hero fails, then the scales of justice will remain imbalanced.

If your hero turns vigilante, exacting justice outside the realms of the law, justice morphs into revenge. For the sake of simplicity, I'll only use the term *justice*, although the principles discussed below apply to both.

The effectiveness of these stakes (as pertaining to the climax) is a function of two factors: (1) the egregiousness of the antagonist's crime, and (2) how much time elapses before the climax commences.

As for the first factor, like with so much of storytelling, it's entirely dependent on context. In action movies, the heinous act often involves the murder of the hero's loved one (*Salt*'s husband), severe bodily harm to the protagonist (Watson in Guy Ritchie's *Sherlock Holmes*), or both (Irene and Holmes in *Sherlock Holmes: A Game of Shadows*).

In the female-driven blockbuster comedies *9 to 5* and *Legally Blonde*, sexual harassment comprises the heinous act. In the sci-fi thriller *Minority Report*, the villain tries to manipulate the hero into committing murder by preying on the hero's grief for his dead son. Nasty, nasty stuff.

With regard to the second factor, the effect of these stakes tends to wane over time. Even when the crime is horrific, if it happens early on in your story, it might not be powerful enough to fire up stakes of justice at the climax.

For this reason, it's usually best for the antagonist to execute his heinous crime right at the end of Act Two, immediately prior to the climax.

As an added benefit, when such a violation occurs at this point, it doesn't just add fuel to your story stakes. It can help you avoid the dreaded "saggy" middle by doubling up as your trough of hell. (This is my term for the setbacks the hero experiences prior to the climax. You might call this the "all is lost" moment. They're the same.)

It may seem rather manipulative to kill off a character just to liven up the middle of your story.

And it is.

But if you want to elicit the maximum degree of emotion from audiences—not just some emotion, but the maximum amount—you have to use a somewhat calculated approach.

Now, I should warn you: using stakes of justice can easily backfire.

Proceed with caution.

If you use too light a touch, if the crime isn't egregious enough, and your hero is especially gung-ho about taking down everyone in his path, the carnage won't emotionally impact audiences the way you may intend.

This is not that common a problem though. More frequently, audiences complain that the writer or filmmaker has gone too far, that the level of violence is gratuitous. They're so appalled, they disengage from the story altogether.

The adaptation of *The General's Daughter* is a good example. The end of the second act concludes with a flashback, specifically to a graphic depiction of rape. Critics of the film felt this violence was excessive and unnecessary.

But to director Simon West, these graphic scenes are vital, and not exploitative. As he explains in the DVD commentary:

> **It's always very tricky with a subject like this. I wanted to be sure that we weren't being exploitative or glorifying the violence. But I also wanted to make sure the scene was horrific enough that you became emotionally engaged in this girl's story, and that the word "rape" wasn't just bandied around as a meaningless crime. You actually had to see how terrible the event was, so that you could sympathize 100% with her, so you understood how big of a betrayal it was when her father let her down and didn't deal with the situation.**

Now that we know both points of view, let's review the events of the film. Its ending consists of three climactic encounters, two of which pit the hero, Paul, against the victim's father, a powerful general.

When the first encounter begins, it seems like the general could have murdered his daughter. On its own, this crime is certainly egregious enough to get audiences emotionally invested in this confrontation.

The horror they witnessed just a few minutes prior heightens this investment, but it's not necessary to generate it. At this point, you could argue that depicting the rape scene is largely unnecessary.

During this confrontation, it transpires that the general did *not* murder his daughter. However, he had covered up the rape in order to protect the reputation of the army. Because audiences witness the horror of the rape themselves, they experience the true extent of the general's betrayal.

Consequently, they want to see the general go down. They want to see him pay. They want to see justice being served.

And it's the intensity of *that* emotion which sustains their involvement in the tail end of this confrontation as well as the entirety of the second one, when, it should be noted, the actual killer has been caught and there's no other standalone stake in play.

If stakes of justice achieved their objective, then the ending would be deeply involving.

If they were absent altogether, then the ending would lack emotional resonance.

If they failed, then audiences would completely disengage.

Simon West decided to take on the risk.

The question is, would you?

Stake Type #11: Hero Happiness

With these stakes, the protagonist has pinned his happiness to a certain "prize."

If he succeeds at the climax, and wins this prize, then his future happiness is ensured. If he fails, he will be devastated.

The prize can be anything; the sky's the limit.

But it pays to be specific.

What does your hero believe will truly make him happy?

If it's an abstract concept like power, success, glory, wealth, or love, then you must define it specifically, linking its acquisition to a concrete object or item audiences can more easily conceptualize, and then, explain to audiences why your protagonist harbors this attitude.

In *The Devil Wears Prada*, Andy defines success as obtaining a prestigious journalism position. This will gain her better "street cred" than her stint at *Runway* magazine. Plus, it will validate her expensive college education as well as her decision to eschew law school—a career path forcefully propounded by her father, who presumably had to foot all those college tuition bills.

Hero happiness, of course, is a part of all the other stakes we've discussed so far. Obviously, a hero's going to be overjoyed about avoiding prison or defying death.

However, two qualities distinguish stakes of hero happiness from the others. Nothing else is at stake besides the hero's future contentment, and furthermore, this contentment is presented as an acquisition of gain rather than the avoidance of loss.

I know, I know. Anything can be couched in different terms.

Gaining love or winning a trophy can be rephrased as avoiding unhappiness. It's a matter of emphasis, and when people think of prizes, sentiment leans toward positive framing.

Generally speaking, heroes pursue a certain prize because it will make them feel better about themselves. When this motivation is underscored, stakes of happiness become especially evocative.

For instance, throughout *Pirates of the Caribbean: The Curse of the Black Pearl*, Captain Jack Sparrow constantly tries to reclaim the *Pearl*.

Why does he pursue her with such passion?

Not because of market value, but manhood.

He must have her back because his self-worth is tied to his possession of the ship. It's an unconventional choice, one of the many that propelled the Pirates of the Caribbean films to the top of the box office.

Incidentally, emphasizing esteem enhances the resonance of all stakes. Unlike Jack, the heroines of *Legally Blonde* and *Miss Congeniality* are not pursuing their climactic goals for their own gratification. Indeed, other stakes dwarf their personal happiness. Even so, their eventual victories are more satisfying to experience because they validate each woman's feelings of self-worth.

Invoking the specter of past trauma is another way to enhance the emotional resonance of stakes of happiness. Audiences will become more emotionally involved in a character's quest, if, in the past, this character has lost the particular prize he seeks in the present.

Juno is a good example. Vanessa Loring tried to adopt a baby before, but in a devastating turnaround, the birth mother reneged on their agreement at the last minute.

This tidbit from Vanessa's backstory isn't dwelled on. It's mentioned once, with only a few lines of dialogue. But this small detail makes the ending, when Vanessa finally gets to hold her baby in her arms, so much more poignant.

In a romance, it's imperative that you show audiences why the hero and heroine can obtain the prize of love only through each other.

You can't just say they are well matched; you have to prove it.

Here's why: if the hero can replace the heroine with another girl, then the loss of the heroine's love shouldn't devastate him (and vice versa). Consequently, stakes of happiness lose their power, and your story will ring hollow.

Let's again return to Andrew and Margaret in *The Proposal*. Andrew's nice, good-looking, and smart. It should be easy for him to find a compatible mate. In fact, his ex-girlfriend, Gert, is a great candidate.

Why should he be with Margaret instead of with his ex?

Gert wants to remain in Alaska. That's why they broke up in the first place. Gert can't support Andrew's personal ambition. Margaret, on the other hand, can. Recognizing that he's in possession of a keen editorial eye, she can support Andrew's aspirations to take over the world of New York publishing.

As for Margaret, Andrew's a perfect match for her as well. He comes with a ready-made family, eager to welcome her into the Paxton clan. Because Margaret is an orphan, this is especially meaningful to her. Plus, with his firsthand knowledge of her own work ethic, Andrew, too, can support her personal ambition.

Show Me the Money (and Something Else)!

While stakes of happiness are always fueled by pursuit of a prize, not all prizes are equal in their ability to elicit audience emotion.

On its own, gaining love is a powerful story stake. As long as the protagonist team plays by the rules, winning a competition can also inspire interest.

Acquiring wealth, however, never works as a standalone story stake. Many beginners fail to understand this.

They forget that in real life, people value money because of what it can provide: safety, freedom, comfort, access, or respect. What's more, they carry over this same attitude to fiction.

If your hero is only in it for the money, audiences are going to be lukewarm about his quest. Although their response will be less tepid if your hero is extremely likeable, that's not enough to sustain emotional involvement in your story.

Either your climax will fall flat, or even worse, audiences will disengage from your story before the climax even begins.

The solution to avoiding these pitfalls is simple: make sure your hero is never in it solely for the money. Make sure his financial gain brings something more to the table than the engorgement of his bank account.

Organized according to common ways the pursuit of wealth manifests itself in stories, the examples below should help illustrate how to accomplish this.

Employment and Promotions

Combining multiple stake types, *Erin Brockovich* sets the gold standard for how to make audiences invest in a protagonist's income. Erin doesn't want to keep her job with Ed Masry's firm to pay for a Netflix subscription. She's a single mother with three kids. She needs the income to provide for them (stakes of livelihood).

As the story progresses, her paycheck takes on additional meaning. It makes her feel like someone important, someone worthwhile (stakes of happiness, with a strong emphasis on self-esteem).

Erin's dedication to her job is not without its costs. She loses her boyfriend over it. Her children grow increasingly resentful of it. And, as we discussed before, she misses out on watching her youngest child say her first word because of it.

For these reasons, the settlement with PG&E means so much more than money. It means that the costs Erin incurred to obtain it were not made in vain (stakes of sacrifice), and furthermore, that the utility has to admit to wrongdoing and pay for it (stakes of justice).

In contrast to *Erin Brockovich*, in some stories, the hero's employment is not tied to any other kind of stake at the film's outset. *Liar Liar* and *Bruce Almighty* are two such examples. In both comedies, Jim Carrey plays a protagonist, who, in the midst of seeking career advancement, is struck by "special powers."

As funny as Fletcher and Bruce's escapades are, if these stories were only about their promotions, audiences would not stick around. They remain emotionally involved because they want to see these heroes choose love over work, to forsake professional heights rather than ascend them.

Recognizing this, by the time their third act climaxes begin, these stories shift gears. In *Liar Liar*, Fletcher's job doesn't play a role at all, while in *Bruce Almighty*, Bruce's workplace rivalry takes a backseat to romance.

This change in focus was critical to the success of both films. If you're working on a project with a high-concept hook similar to theirs, you'll produce a much stronger story if you find a way for your hero's special powers to affect more than his professional aspirations.

Treasure Hunts

On the surface, it would seem that hunts for lost gold or priceless relics would automatically be gripping. They are, after all, exciting, romantic, and lucrative.

Still, they're difficult for audiences to buy into. At the end of the day, they're not going to walk away with the loot.

If you're writing a treasure hunt story, make it easy for readers to invest in your hero's pursuit. Tie his success to a more meaningful set of stakes.

In *National Treasure 2: Book of Secrets*, stakes of reputation initially motivate Ben Gates to search for a lost city of gold. Its discovery would prevent his ancestor's name from being turned "to mud."

In *Romancing the Stone,* Joan Wilder doesn't try to find the *El Corazon* emerald to rent a bigger apartment or fund a shoe addiction. For her, the emerald has nothing to do with creature comforts (stakes of happiness) and everything to do with saving her kidnapped sister (stakes of demise).

Capers and Heists

Like treasure hunts, capers and heists are exciting, romantic, and lucrative. Unlike treasure hunts, they come with an added wrinkle. It's a semantic one, so bear with me.

In a caper or heist, a hero wants to steal a valuable object. The stakes revolve around the acquisition of gain. This is where it gets tricky.

The punishment for failure is usually jail. But in this case, the possibility of a prison sentence is a *risk*.

It does not generate stakes of freedom, which are triggered by *avoiding* imprisonment. In a caper, the hero is not avoiding a prison sentence—he's openly *courting* it in order to acquire money.

In other words, you have to provide audiences with another reason for your hero to risk jail besides the fact that the score will make him really, really rich.

You have to put another stake in play.

The Ocean's trilogy is a good case in point. It's never just about the millions.

In *Ocean's Eleven* (2001), the score is a way for Danny Ocean to steal his ex-wife (and buckets of cash) from the casino mogul dating her.

In *Ocean's Twelve*, when the casino mogul demands remuneration for his losses (plus interest), the score is a way for the protagonists to avoid possible death or "25 to life." (In this situation, since the successful execution of the caper would also enable the crew of con men to *avoid* going to jail, the threat of imprisonment is both a risk and a stake.)

In *Ocean's Thirteen*, the score is about justice. Reuben, one of their own, lost ownership of his casino, suffered a heart attack, *and* became bedridden—all because of an unscrupulous casino mogul (a different one this time). Stealing from this mogul isn't about money, it's about payback.

Yes, Danny Ocean and his men exude likeability and charisma in spades, hearts, clubs, and diamonds. But if you're writing a caper, don't fall into that trap.

It's not enough that your guys are cool. It's not enough that their score is worth big bucks. To write a great caper, you need the trifecta. You need convincing story stakes.

Special Circumstances

Money can be the only stake in play if emotional involvement is supplied by another source. Not likeability (although that certainly is a factor).

In these circumstances, audience investment is usually derived from curiosity about a critical choice to which the entire story has been building.

Out of Sight illustrates this concept very well. Jack Foley wants to steal a stash of uncut diamonds from a smarmy embezzler whom he got to know when they did time together at the state penitentiary.

Because of his criminal record, Foley can't secure honest employment that matches his level of intelligence. The money the diamonds would bring in would enable him to survive while maintaining his self-respect.

But these stakes, as presented in the story, are too weak to keep audiences fully invested in the climax. Their engagement comes from another source: the federal marshal who's hot for Foley—and hot on his tail.

During the heist, audiences know she will have to make a crucial choice. She can either let him go, sacrificing her ethics—or take him into custody, sacrificing their shared attraction.

Picking the latter will raise a new dilemma. Foley has vowed never to go back to prison. If the marshal tries to arrest him, he can comply—and stay alive—or resist, and die free.

Will she—or won't she?

Will he—or won't he?

Wondering the answers to these questions is what makes the climax so gripping.

To put it another way, in a different kind of heist movie, the emphasis would be on whether or not Foley would pull off the heist (because its success is tied to another stake). In this one, the emphasis is on whether or not the federal marshal will let him get away with it.

Villains on the Other Hand…

Villains can be greedy bastards.

They can be in it only for the money, whether it comes in the form of bearer bonds (*Die Hard*), unobtanium (*Avatar*), or soaring pharmaceutical stock (*The Fugitive*).

Just remember this: if the hero fails to achieve his goal, the worst outcome can't be that the villain gets away with his schemes. Audiences don't care if the bad guy then uses his ill-gotten funds to ride off into the sunset and go party in Ibiza.

Well, they may care a little bit, but it's a weak stake. It's not strong enough to sustain emotional involvement in your ending.

Notice that in all of the examples above, there is another, much stronger, stake in play during the climax.

If John McClane fails to stop Hans Gruber in *Die Hard*, McClane's wife will die (stakes of demise). If Sully fails to stop Quaritch in *Avatar*, the entire Na'vi tribe will be in jeopardy (stakes of general protection).

If Kimble doesn't expose Nichols in *The Fugitive*, Nichols will get away not only with murdering Kimble's wife, but also with pinning the murder on Kimble (stakes of justice, among others).

Manufacturing a Mesmerizing MacGuffin

To see how different stake types can interact with each other to create a complex and compelling story, let's take a look at a device closely associated with Alfred Hitchcock: the MacGuffin.

Loosely defined, a MacGuffin is an object in a story which basically every character is searching for. Often used in thrillers, it justifies the actions of the plot.

Several people are pursuing the same thing.

Accordingly, that should generate a lot of conflict.

These same people are willing to engage in chases and fisticuffs in order to secure the MacGuffin.

That should generate a lot of excitement.

Hence, MacGuffins seem like the perfect way to weave together plot, conflict, and thrills. On the surface, at least, that's true.

But take a closer look.

If characters are fighting with one another for no other reason than the plot requires it, no matter how exciting it is, your story will ultimately ring hollow. Audiences will eventually tire of the pointless hijinks and disengage.

This, of course, changes once you bring stakes into the picture. They will add a strong emotional undercurrent to your story. You've still got the same plot, the same conflict, and the same level of excitement, but now you've given audiences *a reason to care about all three.*

To manufacture a mesmerizing MacGuffin, consider using this four-step blueprint:

(1) Select an object with multiple sources of value for your MacGuffin.

That is, the MacGuffin should have the capability to mean one thing to someone, but another thing to someone else.

For example, despite its objective and subjective value, an Olympic gold medal is not likely to make for a good MacGuffin. But if it's been magically imbued with supernatural powers, that might work.

Don't worry if your story doesn't contain paranormal elements. You don't have to resort to magic to create the perfect MacGuffin.

Think of the Neski files in *The Bourne Supremacy*. They mean different things to Jason Bourne, Pam Landy, Ward Abbott, and the Russian oil magnate. (To be clear, this MacGuffin is only in the story briefly, long enough to set up the rest of the plot.)

(2) Determine your roster of "MacGuffin-hunters."

At a minimum, you need two (one protagonist, one antagonist). But the more parties involved, the more conflict your story will contain. So, three is probably the best to start with.

Try incorporating four or more if (a) you're feeling particularly ambitious, or (b) your readers are expecting a story of epic length.

(3) Assign stakes to each of the interested parties.

Ideally, each MacGuffin-hunter is pursuing the MacGuffin for different reasons. (Now you see the importance of step #1.)

Furthermore, at least one of the characters whom you want audiences to root for should be hunting for the MacGuffin for reasons other than financial enrichment.

For instance, one protagonist could be hunting the MacGuffin to save his sister (stakes of demise); another could be hunting it to avoid incarceration (stakes of freedom).

On the other hand, the villain can (but doesn't have to), go after the MacGuffin solely for monetary gain.

Bear in mind that you don't need to introduce every MacGuffin-hunter right off the bat. Just give audiences at least one to root for (someone not driven by purely financial motives, mind you) by the end of Act One.

You can introduce new hunters (and more complications) later on, perhaps at the midpoint.

(4) Finally, design the support system for each of the main MacGuffin-hunters.

MacGuffins typically aren't easy to track down. If they were, the plot would quickly be over. Hence, MacGuffin-hunters enlist helpers to aid them in the search.

These helpers may be in it for the same reasons as the character they're working for, or they could be driven by other motives. Again, variety is ideal.

As an example of what to aspire to, examine the complex and dizzying array of MacGuffin-hunters and helpers in *Pirates of the Caribbean: Dead Man's Chest*.

Further layers of complexity were added to the plot by dividing the MacGuffin—the heart of Davy Jones—into multiple components.

At any given time, a central (or even secondary) character is pursuing Captain Jack Sparrow's compass (which could lead him to the heart); the chest that contains the heart of Davy Jones; the key to the chest that contains Davy Jones's heart; or the heart itself.

The real beauty of it, however, is that a variety of reasons motivate each character.

Take a look (at this somewhat simplified summary):

- Jack wants the heart to call off the deadly Kraken instructed to kill him (stakes of demise).
- Will begins pursuit, at first, to save Elizabeth (stakes of demise), and then later, to liberate his father from the vow his father made to serve Davy Jones (stakes of freedom).
- Elizabeth joins the search, at first, to save Will from the hangman's noose (stakes of demise), and then, later on, to liberate him from Davy Jones's ship (stakes of freedom).
- Norrington eyes the heart to regain his past position (stakes of livelihood) and honor (stakes of reputation).
- Beckett wants the heart to control the seas (stakes of happiness).
- Pintel and Ragetti go after the chest because they've concluded it contains valuable contents (stakes of happiness).
- Davy Jones himself instructs his cursed crew to bring him the chest so he can be assured of the safety of his heart (stakes of demise).

Imagine, for a second, what the film would be like without these stakes.

The breathtaking action would still be there, but the emotional core driving it would be gone. Remember, to be entertained and emotionally involved, audiences require healthy helpings of both.

Generating an enthusiastic response was especially critical for *Dead Man's Chest*, which needed movie-goers to become invested enough to line up in droves to watch the follow-up, *At World's End*.

Speaking of audience involvement, there are ways to modify certain elements of your stakes so that they elicit the greatest degree of emotion.

As a matter of fact, that's the topic of our next chapter...

- chapter two -

8 MODULATING FACTORS WHICH AFFECT THE EMOTIONAL IMPACT OF THE STAKES

IF YOUR STORY INCLUDES ONE OF THE STANDALONE stake types we discussed in the previous chapter, and if you've got a decent handle on writing craft, chances are good that readers will keep turning the pages of your screenplay or novel till they finish it.

But that's not your only goal.

You don't want them to put down your story and promptly reach for another spec script or paperback novel in their TBR pile.

You want them to become so enthralled by their experience that they call everyone they know to tell them to read what you've written.

In short, you want them to transform from casual readers into raving fans.

To do this, you've got to understand that you're judged by one prime standard: the ability to elicit emotion.

Readers rave the most about the tales that make them *feel* the most.

If you keep them under tension, they'll finish your story. But if you keep readers tense *and* deliver a keen, taut emotional experience, once they've finished, they won't be able to keep mum about it.

They will passionately recommend your screenplay or novel to others.

If we place their feelings on a scale of 1–10, you want to be rated an 8 or a 9—and if you've really mastered your craft—even a 10.

For a screenplay, these ratings could mean the difference between a pass and a sale; for a novel, they could mean the difference between a three- or four-star review and a five.

So how do you achieve this level of emotional intensity?

The answer is simple: through modulating factors.

Think of them like the audio control knobs on a stereo system. When used well, modulating factors can turn up "the volume," i.e. the emotional intensity inherently contained within your story stakes.

When used poorly, modulating factors can dial down the emotional intensity, muting audience response to such a degree, it may seem like there are no stakes in play at all!

To put it another way, through modulating factors, audiences will feel more (or less) intensely about *the same set of story stakes*.

Other factors being equal, modulators are the secret to wringing out the extra drop of emotion that will give your story an edge over others in its genre.

They are how you distinguish your save-the-world story from everyone else's.

They are how you set apart your tale of falling in love from all the others like it.

They are how you rise above the competition.

Use their power to your advantage, turn up the emotional volume, and your story should generate the intensity that's required to spark word-of-mouth recommendations—the foundation of a long and profitable career.

For quick reference, here is a list of the eight modulating factors we'll discuss in this chapter:

- the audience-hero bond
- the audience-stake bond
- boundaries and restrictions
- vulnerable populations
- backstory
- setting
- contingency stakes
- the secret modulator

In the introduction to this book, I told you that you couldn't sustain audience interest based on likeability alone. While that's true, likeability is certainly not irrelevant.

In fact, it plays a role in the first modulating factor on our list. Take a closer look…

Modulator #1: The Emotional Bond Between Audiences and the Hero

When a baby duckling hatches from its egg, it imprints on to the first moving object it sees, usually its mother. For a good portion of its life, the duckling will follow whomever it has imprinted on.

And so it goes with audiences. Once they've bonded with a protagonist, they are, metaphorically speaking, willing to follow him wherever he goes.

Unfortunately, unlike ducklings, audiences won't bond with your protagonist just because they've seen him move!

You have to put in a little more effort.

Specifically, you must use cues to signal to them that your hero is either likeable, sympathetic, fascinating…or a combination thereof.

For instance, John and Jeremy in *Wedding Crashers* are both fascinating because of their ability to prey on single women attending weddings. The fact that John is an orphan also makes him sympathetic.

Generally speaking, it's easy to create the audience-hero bond through emotional cues. Unfortunately, it's equally easy to weaken it. When this happens, audience identification with the hero decreases, which in turn, lessens the power of the story stakes.

The two go hand in hand. Stakes are the reason *why* audiences root for your hero; their emotional bond with him affects *how much*.

If the audience-hero bond is strong, audiences are going to care about what the hero does, and whether he succeeds at it or not. If they feel lukewarm toward him, they're going to feel lukewarm toward the stakes.

This is a major problem in stories that only involve stakes of happiness because audiences are only going to care about the hero's potential unhappiness to the extent they care about the hero.

In other stories, while a tepid relationship with the hero isn't a deal-breaker, it's by no means ideal. Since you've reduced the quality of audiences' emotional experience, your story is likely to be eclipsed by the competition that doesn't make this mistake.

To put it bluntly, messing with this bond is bad juju. To avoid wrecking it, watch out for the following:

Emotional Bond Wrecker #1: Too Much Delay

Let's return to our imprinting analogy for a second. The imprinting window is not infinite.

In the case of greylag geese, research conducted by Konrad Lorenz indicates that it's open for about 13–16 hours. [1] During this critical period, if a baby gosling doesn't spot anything moving, it won't imprint on anything at all.

Likewise, you have a limited amount of time to forge a bond between audiences and your protagonist.

In a screenplay, you have about 10 pages. Even though novels are longer, it's still a sound strategy to forge this bond within your first 10 pages. Actually, in both media, it's not a bad idea to forge the bond even sooner—if you can.

If you begin with an exciting genre-fulfilling sequence, there's more flexibility.

Thrillers, for example, commonly open with the villain perpetrating a crime. Although this opening will delay the scene where you show how your hero is likeable, sympathetic, or fascinating, the dynamics continue to work.

Unless you're intentionally (or inadvertently) using bonding cues to muck around with audience loyalty, they'll know they need to hold off. They'll know that you're not asking them to invest in the bad guy.

Even so, they're constantly looking for someone to bond to.

So after you show the villain engaging in his dastardly deed, it's a good rule of thumb to shine your story spotlight on your protagonist, rather than on another character.

The longer you delay introducing your hero, the more likely the audience-hero bond—once it eventually forms—will be weak.

Audiences will still root for your hero, but not as hard as they would have, had you forged the bond sooner.

There's one other element to consider. When you forge a bond between audiences and your protagonist, you create goodwill toward him. This, in turn, generates patience. However, this goodwill (and, correspondingly, patience) dissipates over time.

Even when they've bonded to your protagonist, if audiences don't start to see him pursue a goal—with meaningful stakes attached to it—they will start to fidget. This is one reason why your protagonist should start to go after what he wants by the end of the first quarter of your story.

Think of it like this: sports fans have congregated to watch their favorite team (or player) win the World Series, the World Cup, or the Wimbledon finals. These fans love the players they're rooting for. In fact, they've paid good money just for the privilege to watch these sports matches in person.

But no matter how great their adoration, these fans can't start cheering *until the athletes take the field* and pursue, in earnest, the flag-crested Commissioner's Trophy, the 18-carat gold FIFA trophy, or the silver gilt cup (gentlemen's singles) or the Venus Rosewater Dish (ladies' singles).

The same principle applies to audiences and your hero. Even if they know what and whom they're supposed to root for, audiences can't start to cheer until your hero ventures onto "the playing field."

To root for the hero to stop the bad guy, they have to see the hero take steps to thwart the villain. To root for the heroine to win the hero's heart, they have to see her take steps to woo him. (Or, if the hero and heroine initially resist love, audiences have to see the protagonists go after something else before audiences can root for the hero and heroine to change tack.)

Let's take our analogy one step further. At first, when the sports fans take their seats, they are filled with eager anticipation. But the game doesn't start on time. The longer the delay, the grumpier the fans get.

Their skin gets burned by the sun.

Their muscles become cramped.

They finish their stash of over-priced snacks.

By the time the athletes actually take the field, the enthusiasm of many fans will have waned under the strain of their discomfort and impatience.

Likewise, when you delay past the 25% mark too much, by the time your hero takes steps to achieve his goal, audiences, like overwrought sport fans, will have become grumpy and impatient. This, naturally, withers the bond between them and the hero. Hence, it will be difficult for them to muster enthusiasm for his exploits now.

If you start too early, you'll also run into problems. Premature pursuit definitely comes with drawbacks.

If your hero starts to take steps to achieve his overall goal well before the first quarter-mark, you probably haven't spent enough time establishing the bond between the hero and audiences, between the stakes and audiences (more details on this later), or both. Additionally, you probably have neglected to lay down enough groundwork so that audiences can fully understand and appreciate later events.

Stick to the 25% mark (or thereabouts), and you should achieve just the right balance!

Emotional Bond Wrecker #2: Potential Alienation

Sometimes, it's necessary for protagonists to engage in alienating behavior. This often occurs with unlikeable protagonists, rejected protagonists, or protagonists who have become seduced by power.

You might have to show such protagonists behaving cruelly in order to demonstrate that they're resisting their evolution into better human beings; they're lashing out because of the pain of rejection; or they've become almost unrecognizable due to the effects of power.

Just be careful not to go overboard to illustrate your point.

If your protagonist's behavior is too off-putting, it can destroy the bond between him and audiences to such a degree, that they will not care about his eventual redemption or happiness, i.e. the stakes.

Admittedly, it's tricky to balance the need to show your protagonist's inner turmoil with the need to maintain audiences' connection with him. Here's one quick tip: use mitigating circumstances. They can help smooth the edges, making your protagonist sympathetic even as he indulges in alienating behavior.

For instance, the fact that a female cohost comes onto *Bruce Almighty* (rather than the other way around) removes the sting of his indiscretion. Cady's self-awareness of her own devolution into one of her high school's *Mean Girls* makes her manipulative schemes easier to stomach.

In stories that involve lots of peril, collateral damage can become a major likeability issue. In their quest to save the day, traditional heroes typically inflict pain on others only when absolutely necessary, and, in addition, embrace a "leave no man behind" attitude.

If a hero's actions contradict these values, audiences are likely to divest from him. If the stakes are high, audiences will probably still be emotionally involved in his goal, but this interest will be substantially less than it could have been.

The 2006 remake of *Poseidon* demonstrates this concept perfectly. In one scene, two characters are about to fall into an elevator shaft. One of them, a member of the waitstaff, clings to the other, a successful architect. The architect can be pulled to safety, but only if he shakes off the waiter.

Dylan, another character (and the putative central hero), tells the architect to do it, "to shake him [the waiter] off."

Dylan justifies himself, saying if the architect doesn't shake off the waiter now, both of them will die. Dylan's conclusion appears to be accurate.

Rational, even.

But it's not very heroic.

It makes it enormously difficult to care whether Dylan reaches open water, which, by the way, is the entire plot of the movie! Later, he risks his own life to save another's. But his act of heroism would be infinitely more satisfying if he hadn't acted so callously earlier on.

Granted, it's a disaster flick. More than a few characters are going to perish along the way. Those are the rules of the game. But with all the options available to the filmmakers, surely the waiter could've died in a way that preserves the bond between Dylan and audiences.

In one screenplay draft of *Taken*, in order to gain entrance to an apartment building, Bryan Mills has to bypass a recalcitrant concierge. To accomplish his goal, Bryan knocks the poor Parisian unconscious.

While expedient, the level of violence seems unjustified. The concierge is not about to attack Bryan, he's not working on behalf of the bad guys, and, let's face it, is just trying to do his job.

Naturally, audiences want Bryan to go to the ends of the earth to find his kidnapped daughter. Even so, they're not going to be particularly keen to witness him turn innocent bystanders into collateral damage.

This, after all, is one trait that distinguishes heroes from the bad guys, who are prepared to achieve their objectives by any means necessary.

The movie, fortunately, deviates from the script in this regard. There is no concierge, only a gullible resident who lets Bryan into the building. This change reduces the amount of action in the scene as well as its cinematic appeal.

All the same, the tradeoff is worth it. It preserves the bond between Bryan and audiences, keeping their emotional involvement in his quest at peak levels.

PS: If you're well versed with the film, you might recall that some time prior to the climax, Bryan shoots the wife of a former colleague. Doesn't that count as collateral damage?

Yes—but it's of an acceptable sort.

Here's why: for starters, as Bryan says, it's a flesh wound. (That line of dialogue is pretty crucial.) Plus, his ex-colleague, Jean-Claude, has been taking bribes from the prostitution ring, indirectly enabling the kidnapping. Jean-Claude is, by extension, one of the bad guys, and Bryan's entitled to a little quid pro quo.

Most important, however, is that Jean-Claude can use his resources to tell Bryan to whom the ring sold Bryan's daughter. Bryan desperately needs this information to find her, and Jean-Claude's only going to give it up under duress.

Here, the level of violence is justified.

Emotional Bond Wrecker #3: Dilution of Loyalty
Say that you've introduced your hero to audiences during the critical imprinting window, but that soon afterward, you present other characters to them.

Additionally, these characters are also likeable, sympathetic, or fascinating, and furthermore, share equal screentime with the hero.

What do you think happens then?

Audience investment gets siphoned off into these other characters. Correspondingly, their loyalty to the hero, such that it is, becomes dilute.

In a worst-case scenario, audiences may become confused about whom they should bond with, and, as a result, end up bonding with no one at all.

Hence, audiences will have little interest in the story outcome or the stakes. By the time you reach THE END, their response is neither a cheer, nor a tear, but a "meh." (This is especially true if your story is driven by stakes of happiness.)

To avoid this unwanted outcome, make sure that audiences strongly identify with your protagonist *from the very beginning*.

Use everything at your disposal to tell them that out of everyone they meet, they need to pay attention to *this* guy. Metaphorically, a neon sign should flash above his head that says, "Look at me, bond to me, root for *me*."

If you're writing a screenplay, in addition to bonding cues, evaluate the amount of screentime and dialogue your central protagonist has during the first act. If you're writing a novel, think in terms of point of view (POV), and to a lesser extent, dialogue. As a general rule, your hero should have the lion's share of each.

Here are some more specific tips:

Use the fewest number of characters (or POVs) to tell your story. This will always minimize the potential of diluting audience loyalty to the hero.

Second, try your best to delay introducing new characters (like a sidekick or a love interest) or using a new POV until the end of Act One. Even better, delay it until the beginning of Act Two.

Basically, you want to forge an audience-hero bond that's so strong that even when you ask audiences to invest in other characters, this bond will remain firmly intact.

Keep in mind that you can freely use the villain's perspective without diluting audience loyalty. Again, they know better than to root for the bad guy!

Also, if you're writing a buddy cop comedy or a romance, or a story along those veins, you might elect to create neon signs above *two* protagonists.

But in most cases, for best results, you want audiences to bond strongly with one person during Act One, so that they will care intensely—not tepidly—but intensely about the stakes he will fight for during Act Three.

If, for whatever reason, you absolutely can't delay the introduction of new characters, try to minimize the possibility of confusion.

Ask audiences to invest in *a subset of the cast*.

Although their bond with the characters excluded from this subset will be weak, this is infinitely preferable over audiences feeling apathetic toward all.

If you're writing a screenplay, look at the proportion of your hero's screentime during Act One. Does he have the most in comparison to "the new guys" you introduce along with him? Is it clear that audiences should, out of everyone in the group, focus on him?

If you're writing a novel, have you stayed long enough in your hero's POV to establish that this character is, in fact, the hero… before launching into a new POV?

Don't rely on your book description or series title to provide this information. You can't *tell* audiences to bond with the hero; they've got to *feel* the bond.

If your writing is as gripping as David Baldacci's, you might be able to get away with lots of head-hopping during your opening chapters. But until then, stick to your hero's POV for a significant duration of your novel's beginning.

In this regard, *Ocean's Eleven* (2001) and *The Perfect Storm* are two great movie examples to study. Through the choices the filmmakers made, in *Ocean's*, out of a crew of 11 con men, audiences know to emotionally invest more in Danny (played by George Clooney) and Rusty than in, let's say, the Malloy twins.

In *Storm*, out of a group of six fishermen, audiences know to invest more in Billy (also played by George Clooney) and Bobby than in the guy who has all the luck with the girls (and the one who, unfortunately, does not).

Notice, too, that distinctions are also drawn between Clooney and his primary costar. Audiences are not asked to invest in each man equally. In *Ocean's*, audience loyalty leans more toward Danny than Rusty. Conversely, in *Storm*, between Billy and Bobby, audiences are asked to invest more heavily in the latter.

To sum it up, in the strongest stories, it's always crystal clear to whom audiences should give their allegiance.

One last note, just for screenwriters: according to former MGM executive Stephanie Palmer, focusing on writing "ONE terrific role for a movie star" is a key factor to get agents interested in your script. That's because, in order for agents to sell it easily, it has to have the ability to attract great actors.

"Again, not TWO great roles, but ONE great role," she emphasizes, adding, "A movie star should be thinking, '*This is MY project.*' Otherwise they may be thinking, 'Sure, my role would be great, but who would they cast opposite me and could that person be so amazing that I might be overshadowed?'" [2]

Modulator #2: The Emotional Bond Between Audiences and the Stakes

As we've established, strong emotional identification with your hero is important because it carries over into the stakes.

If the hero cares a lot about the place (stakes of general protection) or person (stakes of demise) he's trying to save, and audiences care about the hero, then by extension, they will care about the stakes.

But to elicit the most intense emotional reaction from audiences, you should forge a bond between them and the stakes that is independent of their bond with the hero.

To do this, employ a two-part strategy. In the first part, focus on creating the bond with the stakes during Act One. In the second part, focus on maintaining this bond throughout Act Two.

If the bond remains strong, when it comes time to save the stakes during Act Three, audiences will be so emotionally invested in them, and so curious about the outcome of the final confrontation, they won't be able to put down your story.

If the bond becomes weak, even though the stakes are in danger, audiences won't be as engaged in their plight as you might anticipate.

Below, we'll cover this topic in greater depth.

Forging the Audience-Stake Bond

If the stakes revolve around the fate of a person, show audiences why the hero would fight tooth and nail to save this individual. If the stakes revolve around the fate of a place, make audiences fall in love with this locale; make them understand why the hero is so passionate about protecting it from harm.

Accomplishing this, fortunately, is simple. You use the same tactics you would use to forge a bond with the hero, primarily bonding cues and screentime.

If you want audiences to care about the love interest who's eventually going to be captured, use bonding cues to make her likeable or sympathetic.

If you want audiences to care about the place that the villain is threatening to destroy, present its residents as likeable or sympathetic.

The prime time to accomplish this objective is during the beginning of your story. Spend as much time as you can with the stakes without bloating your first act to an excessive degree.

Remember, audiences can't start rooting for your protagonist until he actually takes steps to pursue his goal. If you delay for too long (see audience-hero bond wrecker #1), you're only undermining your efforts.

6 Ways to Maintain the Audience-Stake Bond

Stakes usually do not fall into the category of "set it and forget it."

Once you've established a bond between audiences and the stakes, you've got to maintain it. The best way to accomplish this is to periodically remind audiences of what will happen should your hero fail to achieve his goal.

You've got several approaches to choose from. Take a look:

Reminder Strategy #1: No Reminders at All

You may not want to remind audiences about the stakes during Act Two, perhaps because it could affect your story momentum (more on this topic in a bit). If that's the case, it's imperative that the stakes make a memorable impression on audiences during Act One.

To create a strong impression, spend as much time as you can with the stakes in Act One, and make sure that the bonding cues you use really carry their weight!

If the stakes fail to create an impression, when the hero fights to save the stakes during the climax, audiences won't disengage altogether.

But their response will be shallow in comparison to what it could've been, had you created a strong impression during Act

One—or even better, made use of the other reminder techniques discussed below.

Reminder Strategy #2: Symbolic Reminders

Using dialogue by itself to remind audiences about the stakes usually comes across as being too heavy-handed or "on the nose." It's more effective to use dialogue in combination with an image, or perhaps an image alone.

Thus, when you want to remind audiences about the stakes, all you have to do is draw audience attention to an object closely associated with the stakes.

Wedding rings, for example, are used in both *Training Day* and *Face/Off* as reminders that the safety of the hero's family is at stake. Simple and quite effective.

In *Taken*, once Kimmy is abducted, the story doesn't return to her until the very end of Act Two. However, the bond with her, established in Act One, remains strong, mostly due to the use of symbolic reminders.

When she leaves for Paris, Kimmy is wearing a denim jacket with a distinctive bejeweled pattern on its back. When Bryan finds another abducted girl in possession of this jacket, it reminds audiences that Kimmy's fate still hangs in the balance.

Additionally, even though Kimmy herself is in danger, she is kind enough to give her jacket to this other girl. This act of compassion functions as a "likeability booster," reinforcing the bond between her and audiences even further, and making them even more invested in Bryan's mission to rescue her.

That's not all. The film uses another, more tragic symbol as a reminder. Kimmy is abducted at the same time as her best friend. Bryan manages to locate this girl. She's dead, having choked on her own vomit.

It's a sinister reminder of what could happen to Kimmy if Bryan doesn't find her before time runs out. Because audiences witness the negative consequences of failure occur to another character but not to Kimmy herself, I think of this as a "surrogacy" reminder.

For a more comedic variation of a surrogacy reminder, we can revisit *Pirates of the Caribbean 2*. Bootstrap Bill warns Jack that the monstrous Kraken is coming for Jack and the *Black Pearl*. Soon thereafter, a fisherman finds Jack's cap floating in the water.

The cap acts like a homing beacon, luring the Kraken to the unfortunate fisherman's boat. The monstrous beast destroys the vessel—and all onboard—instantly. Because audiences see what Jack fears will happen to him, happening to *other* characters, the stakes feel more real and intense than if audiences didn't have this experience at all.

Reminder Strategy #3: Chaotic Reminders

To make use of this reminder strategy, you simply show audiences the potential damage the antagonist could inflict upon the stakes.

If he's threatening to destroy a city, for instance, you could show the villain causing traffic jams on all the major roads and highways. Although this would be detrimental to several citizens (and emergency vehicles in particular), it's only a hint of the malicious destruction the villain intends to inflict upon the population at the climax.

When stakes of demise are involved, villains often bully or belittle the person they've taken captive. Similar to our traffic jam example, while unpleasant, it's only a hint of what's to come. Since this behavior is so despicable, when the story switches focus from the stakes and returns back to the hero, audiences root even harder for the hero to succeed.

If the captive responds to the villain's taunts with courage, this bravery also functions as a likeability booster, which again, makes audiences even more invested in the hero's rescue mission.

In a variation of the chaotic reminder, the villain can remind the hero what the hero stands to lose, should he fail to follow the villain's instructions. In *Training Day*, for example, Alonzo spins a hypothetical scenario, which will unfold should Jake fail to cooperate with Alonzo's plan:

"A Los Angeles police department narcotics officer was killed today, serving a high-risk warrant in Echo Park," Alonzo says and points a gun at Jake. "LAPD spokesperson said the officer is survived by his wife and infant child. You get the picture?"

Reminder Strategy #4: Subplot Reminders

Here's another way to remind audiences about the stakes: integrate them into the fabric of your story through a subplot.

In other words, the character who comprises the stakes will pursue his own goal, which is distinct from the protagonist's overall goal, but nevertheless, intersects with it somehow.

To see how this works, let's return to our hypothetical traffic jam from reminder strategy #3. The villain has created a huge pileup on one of the city's major roads. A local patrolwoman is doing her best to disentangle the mess.

The story flits between showing the hero's actions to stop the villain (the plot) and the patrolwoman's actions to restore order to the streets (the subplot).

While her actions are compelling in their own right—at one point the patrolwoman rescues a child trapped inside of a minivan—they are occurring in parallel to the hero's actions (which should take precedence).

Their storylines haven't crossed yet—and they won't—not until later on…when it's revealed she's actually the hero's wife, the villain has made this discovery, and accordingly, takes her hostage.

Audiences will be especially riveted by the climax, not just because the situation has gotten extremely personal for the hero, with whom they strongly identify, but also because they've bonded to the stakes. They've spent enough time with the patrolwoman that, *irrespective of their bond with the hero*, they care about what happens to her.

In this example, the intersection of the subplot and the main plot was supposed to be a surprise for readers. They have spent time bonding with the stakes, *without truly realizing it*. When done well, this can be a great plot twist.

All the same, you don't have to be so subtle with this reminder strategy. You can integrate a stake subplot whose intersection with the main plot is quite clear. When audiences spend time with the stakes, they know full well that these are the stakes of the story.

The Perfect Storm begins and ends with Bobby, who wants to build a new life with his girlfriend and her children. Before he leaves the harbor, she slips a note into his bag. In it, she tells him that she has a surprise for him. She's gotten them a house. It's not much, but it's a start.

On the surface, showing her fixing up this old house may seem like a waste of time. But these scenes were included for a reason. Bobby's girlfriend, and their future together, are the regret-tinged stakes of the story. (Part of them, at any rate.)

They add extra emotional weight to Bobby's survival. It isn't just a matter of him staying alive. It goes beyond that: if he lives, he can enjoy the happy home life he always dreamed of.

Audiences, too, look forward to the intersection of the subplot and the main plot, of him returning back to shore and joyfully discovering the home his girlfriend has created with so much love.

Unfortunately, Bobby doesn't make it. No one on his boat does.

However, his death is the most poignant of them all. This is partly due to screentime—Bobby has a huge proportion of it. But it's also due to the stakes attached to his survival.

When he dies, audiences feel sorrow not just because of his death but also because they have experienced firsthand the future he has been deprived of. It is not vague or amorphous; it is concrete and real.

Remove the mini-subplot from the story, and Bobby's death, while still tragic, wouldn't be as emotionally resonant.

Reminder strategy #4 is also effective when coupled with strategy #3. That is, you not only show the villain menacing the person he has taken hostage, but in addition, you give the captive person his own subplot, his own agenda.

This usually entails showing the captive repeatedly attempting to escape his captor. Again, this bravery also boosts the captive's quotient of likeability, making audiences root very strongly for his survival.

Reminder Strategy #5: Ride-Along Reminders

In this reminder strategy, the stakes accompany the hero on his Act Two journey. This is often the case when the person whose life is at stake during the climax is a teammate or sidekick of the hero, or alternately, is someone whom the hero is assigned to protect.

As the story progresses, through screentime and bonding cues, audiences get to know the stakes quite well. Thus, it's possible to squeeze creation and maintenance of the audience-stake bond entirely within the second act of your story.

This is a great option to explore if, for whatever reason (time restraints, story structure, etc.), you can't introduce the stakes during Act One.

In *Speed*, the hostages on the bus are ride-along stakes who literally go on a high-octane ride along with the hero! Of all of the hostages, audiences get to know Annie the best. In fact, to highlight her importance, the film takes the time to show her boarding the doomed bus (in a dramatic way too!).

Although the other hostages are accorded lesser importance, not all recede into the background. The film periodically shines a spotlight on a subset of them: the bus driver, the annoying tourist, and the guy who compliments Jack's *cajones*. That way, audiences can form a bond with this cohort, and correspondingly, remain emotionally invested in the plight of the group as a whole.

For a less literal example of ride-along stakes, examine *Ghost*. During the beginning of the story, audiences connect with the hero and heroine, Sam and Molly. Later on, during Act Two, Sam, now a ghost, recruits a psychic, Oda Mae Brown, to help him communicate with Molly from beyond the grave.

Due to the screentime Oda Mae shares with Sam and Molly (in addition to Oda Mae's vivacious personality), audiences develop a bond with her, which is distinct from their bond with the protagonists.

At the climax, the villain and his associate make their final play and try to kill Molly and Oda Mae. These sequences are gripping in and of themselves, but they're even *more* riveting because audiences have gotten to know, and like, both women.

Reminder Strategy #6: Intra-Climax Reminders

During the climax, don't just show the hero battling the villain. Remind audiences why this battle matters in the first place.

Cut away to the stakes, whose fate is about to be decided once and for all. (*Note*: This is slightly easier to implement in a screenplay than in a novel.)

It seems like an obvious strategy, but surprisingly, it's often overlooked. Many writers go through the trouble of establishing the stakes, and then neglect to bring them to the forefront at the climax, when their presence is going to have the most impact.

If audiences haven't gotten to know the stakes, cutting away to them during the climax can still be effective (particularly when you make use of modulating factors #3 and #4; more details forthcoming). But audiences' emotional response is going to be much more intense when they've bonded with the stakes throughout the course of your story.

Reminders and Momentum

When you're evaluating the reminder strategies discussed above, make sure you take momentum into account.

The actions a hero takes in order to stop his antagonist have a strong forward trajectory. Stakes, on the other hand, usually don't have this kind of energy.

They tend to be suspended in stasis, waiting for the villain to make his next move. So when you switch from the hero's actions to focus on the stakes, your story momentum can seriously stall.

Reminder strategies #1, #2, and #5 (no, symbolic, and ride-along reminders) tend to affect momentum the least. They are especially good to employ when your story takes place within a tight time frame. Reminder strategies #3, #4, and even #6 (chaotic, subplot, and intra-climax reminders) have the most potential to derail the momentum of your story.

Generally speaking, the more momentum you can infuse within the scenes involving the stakes, the less you'll hurt the momentum of your story as a whole as you flit between the two.

In our hypothetical example, the patrolwoman isn't just waiting around, stuck in traffic. She has her own agenda and is busy saving others. Her activity carries with it, its own forward trajectory. It might not have the same force as the main plot, but it is something.

Tension is another factor to consider. If audiences are extremely worried about the safety of the stakes, they will be so distracted, they won't realize that the momentum has almost come to a standstill.

In *The Silence of the Lambs*, the film occasionally switches from focusing on Clarice's search for a kidnapped woman to focusing on the young woman herself. Far from dissipating the momentum, these tense scenes recharge audiences' emotions. When the story returns back to Clarice, they are even more invested in her quest to save the young woman in time.

Modulator #3: Boundaries and Restrictions

If your protagonist has infinite tries to accomplish his goal, things are going to get boring pretty fast. That's because, in this situation, there really aren't any consequences of failure.

If your hero doesn't succeed, he can pick himself up, dust himself off, and try—and try and try and try—again.

While the stakes of your story will still be present, without limits, they lack tension. They've got no edge, no bite.

If you want to ratchet up the tension and increase the power of your story stakes, tighten the restrictions surrounding your hero. Three possible arenas to explore include:

- time
- resources
- magic

Time

In real life, deadlines create stress, which in turn, evokes the "fight or flight" response. When activated, this physiological mechanism produces a cascade of hormones that increase blood pressure, pulse rate, and rapidity of breath.

Sounds like tension city to me.

To your great advantage, fictitious deadlines, like their real-life counterpart, have the power to elicit a strong emotional response from audiences. If your hero is under stress, they're under stress. They're stewing in a big fat vat of story tension.

Bingo! Exactly what you want.

This is why ticking clocks are so popular. Taking deadlines to the extreme, they often leave the hero with mere minutes—or seconds—to achieve his goal. They're one of the simplest ways to increase the potency of whatever story stakes are already in play.

Although you can use a literal clock to cinematically depict your hero's deadline (the tolls of Big Ben are a nice touch in *Sherlock Holmes* (2009)), there are certainly other options.

Declining levels of fuel, for instance, are used to increase tension in *Speed*, *Air Force One*, and *Die Hard 2*. Also, the rose petals in Disney's *Beauty and the Beast* create an elegant alternative to a physical clock.

Here's another option: create a ticking clock through the completion of a process that yields a visible result. Once the result is produced, your protagonist will be out of time.

In "Digging Deeper," episode eight from season five of *White Collar*, Neal must catch a collector who illegally obtains artifacts. To do so, Neal sells the collector a fake dinosaur egg. Before handing over payment, the collector X-rays the egg with a CAT scanner.

The closer the machine gets to producing a full rendition of the egg's interior—revealing that it doesn't, as it should, contain a dinosaur embryo—the less time Neal has to extricate himself from his precarious situation.

Thinking in terms of proximity instead of time can help too. In *Batman Begins*, the closer and closer the monorail comes to Wayne Tower, the less time Batman has to stop mass deployment of a hallucinogen that will drive Gotham's citizens insane.

In *Taken*, Bryan must track, and then sneak onto, a fancy boat carrying his kidnapped daughter, before it reaches open water.

A small-scale (and decidedly more comedic) version of this concept can also be found in *27 Dresses*.

If you're writing a romantic comedy, be careful. Avoid the dreaded cliché of having your hero or heroine race to the airport during the climax. By the same token, don't throw out the baby with the bathwater.

Keep the urgency (the race); jettison the cliché (the airport).

Notting Hill is a good model to study. Initially, screenwriter Richard Curtis had planned for Will to race to the airport to plead his case with Anna before she leaves England for good. Happily, producer Duncan Kenworthy persuaded Curtis to drop the cliché.

Instead, Will races *to a hotel* where Anna is holding a press conference prior to her stateside departure. While the dynamics of the sequence are fundamentally the same, the change in venue makes all the difference. With this simple tweak, Curtis kept the urgency, but lost the triteness. (As a side note, if you regularly struggle with the race-to-the-airport cliché, you can find a step-by-step approach to tackle it in my writing guide, *Story Climax*.)

Bear in mind, to intensify the stakes, you don't have to use time only as a ticking clock. If you modify your protagonist's "starting position," so that he begins your story during a milestone in his life, you may also be able to elicit a deeper degree of emotion from audiences.

Career setbacks and romantic mishaps, for instance, may not bother a heroine at all when she's in her early twenties. She's got plenty of time to get her life on track. But circumstances that are tolerable at age 25—even 29—may feel unbearable, downright insurmountable, once she's hit 30 (a milestone birthday). Perhaps, this situation causes her to go to extreme lengths for the sake of stakes of happiness or livelihood.

Similarly, if a detective, having been accused of corruption, is cleared of all charges and returns to work, he's got more to prove on his first case back (a milestone assignment). Whether stakes of general protection, demise, or justice are involved, failure now is going to carry a higher toll than if his professional integrity had never been questioned.

Resources
Machine guns may keep the level of action high, but they have a major drawback. Barring other factors, they keep the tension low.

If the hero misses his mark, it's not a big deal. He's got plenty more ammo to go.

But if your hero has only one bullet left to kill or injure the villain, you've got the makings of an ultratense showdown.

In a nutshell, limiting the resources at your hero's disposal increases the intensity of audience response.

This is especially true at the climax. In *Twister*, two tornado chasers start off with four data-gathering machines (which they've nicknamed Dorothy). By the time the climax begins, they're down to one. This is their last chance to insert the Dorothy machine into a tornado, a feat which will enable them to glean the data necessary to create an improved forecasting system.

See how this situation impacts the climax? If the tornado chasers still had all four Dorothy machines at the climax, it would hardly be thrilling. The depletion of this resource heightens the tension. Same stakes, different restriction, different results.

In stories that involve a courtroom climax, the judge's store of patience is often presented as a limited resource. Typically, audiences are made to believe that the protagonist better make his point quickly before the judge runs out of patience and sends the poor protagonist packing.

Naturally, combining a ticking clock with depleting resources will double up the tension, making your story all the more gripping.

In *Star Wars: A New Hope*, for instance, the rebels must destroy the Death Star before it comes within firing range of their planet (the ticking clock). Their odds of success, however, decrease as their squad of fighter planes diminishes (depleted resources).

Returning to *Notting Hill*, Will must guess Anna's cartoon alias from a concierge before the concierge runs out of patience (depleted resources). If Will doesn't accomplish this goal in time, as aforementioned, he won't be able to find her and woo her back before she leaves the country (ticking clock).

Magical Powers

Let me share with you a brief fairy tale:

Once upon a time, a princess lived in a beautiful kingdom with her little sister, whom she adored. Things were great, until the princess had to visit some out-of-town relatives.

A jealous dragon took this opportunity to kidnap the princess's little sister. When the princess returned to her kingdom and discovered the news, she immediately left her home to save her sibling.

Unbeknownst to the dragon, at her relatives' house, the princess had imbibed tons of whey protein shakes, which magically boosted her immunity to dragon's breath and dragon fire.

The princess raced to the dragon's lair and…and…and…

…do you really care?

There's no danger here, no tension at all. This is a complete and utter snooze fest.

But what if things were different?

What if whey protein shakes give the princess some prized magical power, but, as a peculiar side effect, they make her even *more* vulnerable to dragon's breath and dragon fire?

Even with her newfound paranormal capability, because of her concurrent newfound weakness, when the princess races to the dragon's lair, she's in more danger than before. The stakes remain the same—the little sister must be saved—but the tension is considerably amplified.

That's all due to the power of limits. Learn to love them!

When you first create your sorcerer or superhero, have a blast developing his magical abilities or special powers. But when you're done, make sure you spend an equal amount of time reflecting on the limits of his preternatural talents.

And when you've finished with *that*, figure out how you're going to clearly communicate those limitations to your reader—without slowing down your story with the expository details.

Notice that the effect is different with antagonists. If a villain is all-powerful, when the hero comes to fight him, the tension doesn't diminish.

It will escalate to an almost unbearable peak. Audiences will most definitely be riveted.

Nevertheless, you still have to devise some sort of limit to the villain's power, create some chink in his armor.

If you don't, your hero's eventual victory is going to come across as contrived and unbelievable. You'll end up with a dissatisfied audience—the very thing you're trying to avoid!

Modulator #4: Vulnerable Populations

There's a reason videos of babies and animals go viral so quickly. A scientific reason, no less.

According to evolutionary biology, humans are hardwired to respond to cuteness. Juvenile characteristics instinctually arouse feelings of protectiveness and affection.

These features include: a large head, wide eyes, round cheeks, flabby limbs, and awkward movements—basically, as a *New York Times* article by Natalie Angier summarizes, anything that indicates "extreme youth, vulnerability, harmlessness, and need." [3]

As the theory goes, these juvenile characteristics produce instinctual reactions that compel adults to take care of their babies, thereby ensuring the survival of the species.

Curiously enough, although these instincts evolved to protect human offspring, they can be evoked by virtually anything with cute features. As Angier puts it, "The human cuteness detector is set at…a low bar."

What does this mean for you, as a screenwriter or novelist?

Well, this means that when you use a member of a vulnerable population (e.g. a child or a pet), as story stakes, you'll be tapping into a hardwired, instinctive source of empathy.

You don't have to use bonding cues to manufacture it; it's automatically produced, and presumably, the stronger of the two. When used in conjunction with each other, you should be able to elicit an extraordinary degree of emotion from audiences.

The question is…should you?

You have your own personal threshold of how much child (or animal) endangerment you can handle. Audiences, likewise, have their own.

If you go beyond what they can tolerate, you'll end up with the exact opposite of what you were aiming for. Audiences will become so horrified, they will completely disengage from your story. You'll have to rely on your own storytelling instincts, good judgment, and knowledge of your genre to achieve a happy medium.

You might not be comfortable with the idea of putting children or animals in harm's way at all. That's fine. You can completely ignore this modulating factor altogether…or you can modify it so it conforms to your level of comfort.

For instance, instead of directly putting children in danger, you can hint at the dark fate they will face should the heroes fail. This is done to excellent effect in the Battle of Helm's Deep at the climax of *The Two Towers*.

In between depicting the action taking place outside the fortress, director Peter Jackson employed reminder strategy #6 and cut away to caverns sequestering women and children. Unlike the soldiers, these innocents are not directly in harm's way, but instead, are one-step removed from it. Still, their presence reminds audiences why the battle matters.

There's another option as well. Put only adults in danger, but—and here's the key—make them as innocent and childlike as possible.

Look at *Miss Congeniality*. If Gracie is not successful in apprehending a malicious saboteur, all the contestants in the beauty pageant could die. The film humanizes these general stakes by highlighting Gracie's interactions with a specific subset of girls.

Out of this cohort, one girl is further emphasized: Cheryl, the most artless and unworldly of the bunch. In other words, the most childlike.

You can see this same pattern in *Knight and Day*. During one part of the climax, the hero has to rescue a young genius, who exhibits endearingly boyish enthusiasm for trains, code messages, and the musical duo Hall & Oates.

As a side note, this genius invented an infinitely renewable battery, the MacGuffin of the story. Intriguingly, an early draft of the script (back when it was entitled *Wichita*), features the battery, but doesn't include its geeky inventor.

The film version took the stakes up several notches by tying the MacGuffin to an actual person whom—unlike an inanimate object—audiences can bond with, and scored even more bonus points by making this person boyish and childlike!

Modulator #5: Hero Backstory

Create connective threads between your hero's past experiences and present situation, and you'll add an extra layer of intensity to whatever stakes are already in play.

To take advantage of the power of backstory, there are two major methods you can adopt. In the first method, the current plot should be constructed in such a way that it echoes an incident from the hero's past.

We've already seen this with stakes of regret (which emphasize redemption). The possibility of success (or failure) in the present is more emotionally resonant in these stories because the hero failed to accomplish something similar in the past.

But backstory can be used for purposes other than to create a redemptive plot. In romance novels, such as *The Duchess War* by Courtney Milan, it can be used to intensify the scope of a protagonist's betrayal.

Through the heroine's backstory, readers learn that her father betrayed her during a courtroom trial. At the climax, the hero must betray the heroine—during a courtroom trial—in order to save his brother. Thus, the hero's betrayal in the present is greatly magnified because of its similarity to the betrayal the heroine experienced at the hands of her father in the past.

If you want to implement the same technique, you could start with backstory, and then purposefully construct the climax so that it mirrors the past in key respects.

Alternately, you could examine the plot you've already constructed, and then modify your protagonist's backstory to strengthen the similarities between the two.

In the second method, to take advantage of backstory, you focus less on the design of the plot and more on the shared history of key characters.

Take the average murder case, for instance. Failure to solve it is going to seem worse if the investigator knew the victim's father (like Murtaugh in *Lethal Weapon*) than if the victim were someone the investigator had no prior connection to at all.

Likewise, in a spy thriller, the stakes will feel higher if the hero has to rescue a colleague who's known to him (perhaps his protégé, as in *Mission: Impossible III*), rather than someone he's never interacted with before.

In save-the-world stories, it's a nice touch for the hero to share a connection with the villain, rather than have the villain emerge, fully formed, from out of nowhere, almost like Athena borne from the forehead of Zeus.

The threads that link Kirk and Spock to Nero in *Star Trek* (2009) make the plot much more interesting than if the heroes hadn't had any prior dealings with Nero.

In both *Star Wars* and *Kung Fu Panda*, the connective thread is wrought through the hero's mentor, who also trained the villain. The irony of it all gives these stories an extra edge.

And, of course, in a romance, the breakup of the hero and heroine (before the happy ending) will be more poignant if they had been romantically (and tragically) entangled in the past.

Naturally, every character can't share history with your protagonist. Nor should he.

But it's always good practice to ask yourself if adding a pre-existing relationship between key characters would enhance the emotional resonance of the stakes.

On top of this benefit, hinting at backstory, without revealing it fully, is another great way to keep readers turning the pages!

Modulator #6: Setting

In certain settings, the consequences of failure can appear to carry, or actually do carry, more weight than they would in a different milieu.

To put it another way, by virtue of the world he inhabits, a character may have further to fall. Hence, setting is our sixth modulating factor.

Test this theory out. Take whatever plot you've got, transfer it to a glamorous setting, and watch as the stakes miraculously become higher.

As an example, consider this premise: a local politician is up for reelection. A widower, he's starting to date an environmental lobbyist.

This has the makings of a classic romance novel. Not bad. But what happens if we transplant this politician into the world of Washington, D.C.?

The president of the United States is up for reelection. A widower, he's starting to date an environmental lobbyist.

We've changed one detail—the setting—and raised the stakes so high that we now have a plot for a high-concept romantic comedy. (In fact, it's the basis of *The American President*.)

As a starting point, these worlds are all popular, high-stake settings:

- national (or international) governments
- royal kingdoms

- the Hollywood film and TV industry
- lifestyles of rock stars and other high-profile musicians
- competitive sports (at the professional level)

Although these settings are tried and true, any place where money, prestige, and power comingle can be a prime candidate.

That being said, not every story has to have a glamorous backdrop to be compelling. The world of suburbia (as in Liane Moriarty's *The Husband's Secret*) is also rich and complex. However, in low-key settings, you usually have to work harder to make your story stakes feel high.

Modulator #7: Contingency Stakes

Of all the stakes listed in the first chapter of this book, some cannot stand alone and operate by themselves.

While these stakes imbue the hero's climactic victory with extra significance, they are not the reason why the hero goes on his journey.

They are stakes of:

- regret
- suffering
- sacrifice

Because they are dependent upon the other stake types, collectively, they can be grouped together in one category. I refer to them as contingency stakes.

At first, you may think that contingency stakes are rather useless since they can't operate by themselves. But it's unwise to discount them right off the bat because they do have the power to affect audience response to the stakes that *can* stand alone.

In short, contingency stakes can make audiences feel more (or less) emotionally involved with standalone stakes—the very definition of a modulating factor.

Stakes of regret and sacrifice tend to transform a concept that's already strong into something exceptional. Their absence won't necessarily ruin a story, but their inclusion will greatly enhance it.

Stakes of suffering, on the other hand, need to be included in *all* stories.

When the hero doesn't suffer enough during Act Two, audiences tend to feel ambivalent toward the story's ending. No matter how hard the hero fights at the climax, it will seem like he doesn't quite deserve to win, that he doesn't truly deserve his reward.

This holds true, regardless of what other stakes are in play. Whether someone's happiness or someone's life is at stake, audiences are going to be more invested in the outcome of the climax if the hero had to overcome impossible odds to even reach this stage.

Oh, and if you want to know how to make your hero really suffer at the end of Act Two, check out my writing guide, *Trough of Hell*. It will give you solid pointers on how to put your hero through the wringer, thereby avoiding the dreaded "saggy" middle!

Modulator #8: The Secret Modulator

There's one last modulating factor to add to our list, but it's best understood within the scope of the following chapters, which explore the story stake matrix.

What is this mysterious matrix all about?

Unlike Neo, you don't need to pop a red pill to find out. Just turn the page to learn more...

NOTES

1. Wikipedia, s.v. "Imprinting (psychology)," last modified July 14, 2015, https://en.wikipedia.org/wiki/Imprinting_(psychology).

2. Stephanie Palmer, "How to Write a Screenplay Agents Will Love," *Good in a Room* (blog), June 4, 2014, http://goodinaroom.com/blog/how-to-write-a-screenplay-agents/.

3. Natalie Angier, "The Cute Factor," *New York Times*, January 3, 2006, http://www.nytimes.com/2006/01/03/science/03cute.html.

- chapter three -

THE STORY STAKE MATRIX: GROUNDWORK

IT'S TIME TO ADDRESS A SALIENT POINT WE HAVEN'T really touched on before: the stakes can't remain the same throughout your story.

To sustain audience involvement, the negative consequences of failure have to grow. They have to escalate.

This, as you can guess, poses a conundrum. If you start with stakes that are "low" enough to give you room to grow, then your initial premise might not be compelling enough to garner audience interest in the first place.

But, if you start out with stakes that are high, it will be difficult to make them worse (and, by extension, keep audiences interested) as your story progresses.

This is where the story stake matrix comes in. It pulls everything—stake types and modulating factors—together.

With this tool, you'll be able to:

- use stakes and modulating factors to craft a premise with more commercial appeal
- raise the stakes (even when they're already high)
- avoid an anticlimactic ending

However, to fully understand it, we have to cover a little more groundwork, starting with the hierarchy of needs.

The Hierarchy of Needs

As described in psychologist Abraham Maslow's 1943 article "A Theory of Human Motivation" published in *Psychological Review*, human behavior is driven by five basic needs:

- physiological (the need for food, water, sleep, oxygen, etc.)
- safety (security of the body or family unit, health, employment)
- belongingness & love (romantic, platonic, familial)
- esteem (self-confidence, self-respect, respect from others)
- self-actualization (realization of a person's full potential)

This overview is just a springboard for everything to follow. To be clear, from here on out, I'm modifying Maslow's hierarchy to suit our purposes.

First, we're going to disregard physiological needs as well as self-actualization, leaving us with safety, belongingness & love, and esteem.

Second, we're going to group the need for belongingness & love with the need for esteem. I refer to this group as spiritual needs because they satisfy one's soul.

Real life would be wretched without the fulfillment of spiritual needs. All the same, this fulfillment becomes a moot issue when basic requirements for survival are not met. Indeed, in times of crisis, spiritual needs often become a luxury.

Therefore, in our framework, spiritual needs do not share the same degree of importance as safety needs.

Third, we're going to introduce a new category to Maslow's original hierarchy: contingency needs.

Their distinguishing trait is that they make people feel better about the choices they've made in the past. To repeat a point from a previous chapter, although contingency needs imbue the outcome of your story's climax with extra meaning, they are not the reason why your hero embarks on his journey.

Like spiritual needs, if met, contingency needs improve the overall quality of one's life. But they're still moot when someone's having difficulties surviving.

Based on the needs they satisfy, story stakes can be classified into one of these three categories:

Safety Need Stakes

- general protection
- demise

- livelihood
- freedom
- reputation (when tied to another safety need stake)
- sanity
- access (depends on context; perhaps it involves integrity of the family unit or ownership of a home)

Spiritual Need Stakes

- reputation (when not tied to a safety need stake)
- access (again, it depends on context; perhaps it involves loss of contact with a romantic prospect)
- justice
- hero happiness

Contingency Need Stakes

- regret
- suffering
- sacrifice

Before we can use these definitions to construct our matrix, we have to address one more parameter: the cost of hero participation.

The Cost of Participation

The cost of participation comprises all the dangers associated with the tasks a protagonist must complete in order to achieve his goal. The cost can be high, or it can be low.

High vs. Low Costs

Activities that threaten your protagonist's life (body or soul), freedom, or means of survival are high cost.

Activities that threaten his esteem, putting him at risk of humiliation or embarrassment, are low cost. Activities that merely consume time or resources, but that are not inherently dangerous, are also low cost.

Tone plays a factor too. If the dangerous activities are played for laughs, they are still low cost.

For instance, in both *Speed* and *Miss Congeniality*, Sandra Bullock's character tries to save others from being killed by an explosive device. In the former, the danger to her own life is grave (high cost); in the latter, her personal jeopardy is humorous (low cost).

The same principle applies to authority figures. In comedies, although a protagonist might have to "battle" with them, to maintain the humor, authority figures (like the police officers in *Horrible Bosses* or the immigration official in *The Proposal*) do not exude true menace.

One final point about costs: loss of employment can go either way. It depends on how you present it.

If your hero has to sacrifice his promotion to get the girl, that's a low-cost activity. If he has to put his employment at risk, but he doesn't have anyone else depending on his income, and there's a sense that he'll land safely on his feet, then again, his sacrifice will be low cost.

On the other hand, if he's a neurosurgeon, the star actor in a Broadway musical, the leader of the free world—basically anyone who has invested a lot of time and energy to score a rare career opportunity—then his sacrifice will be high cost.

If it seems unlikely that he'll be able to find employment elsewhere, giving up his current job will also be high cost.

Cost vs. Stakes

On the surface, it may appear that stakes and the cost of participation are one and the same.

But they're not.

We actually touched on this issue earlier, when we talked about capers in the "Show Me the Money" section in the first chapter. Here, we'll go into more detail. Like with the caper example, this will get a little semantic, so bear with me.

To start our explanation, we're going to develop an imaginary scenario. It features a hero named Bobby. In order to cross the street, Bobby has to navigate through oncoming traffic. The drivers are either in a rush or are too busy texting to pay attention to the road.

They're not going to stop for Bobby, so crossing the street puts his life in danger. However, his life is *not* at stake…because Bobby can walk away from the situation. He doesn't have a compelling reason to face these hazards.

This changes when we tinker with the details and give Bobby a reason why he cannot walk away.

If he's being pursued by a *Tyrannosaurus rex*, and there's a tranquilizer gun on the other side of the street, Bobby has to face the danger of oncoming traffic and risk his life, in order to (hopefully) save it.

If he's feeling particularly bold, Bobby may also stand his ground and challenge the *T. rex* to an epic wrestling match, which will end the reptile's pursuit once and for all. Although the danger's different—Bobby's risking the dinosaur's powerful jaws and claws rather than careless drivers—his motivation is still to save his life.

One more variation: if Bobby's wife is being held hostage on the other side of the street, and if Bobby crosses it, he just might be able to save her, then he's putting his life in danger because hers is at stake.

We can modify our scenario to include low-cost participation as well. The drivers won't stop for Bobby, but he can laugh off any bruises, bumps, or wounds he incurs en route to the other side of the street.

Alternately, there's no oncoming traffic at all. Drivers will readily stop for Bobby. But he has to trip on a banana peel while voicing his deepest fears and greatest dreams.

Did I mention he's naked?

In either situation, all the drivers observing Bobby's predicament will laugh loudly at him, but if Bobby faces their ridicule, he'll get a prize—like the love of a good woman—that'll more than make up for it.

Why Does This Distinction Even Matter?

This isn't just a bunch of semantics, which only word nerds will enjoy. There is a point to it.

And here it is: when the cost of participation rises for your hero—when he's got to put more skin in the game—the negative consequences of failure get worse.

This has the net effect of raising the stakes, *even though, technically, the stakes actually remain the same.* In fact, the cost of participation is—ta-dah!—our eighth, and last, modulating factor. It's one you will routinely employ to deepen audience involvement with your story.

BUT (and yes, it really needs to be in all uppercase letters) increasing the cost of participation, i.e. increasing the dangers to your hero, only works if these dangers match the stakes *already* in play. If they aren't in alignment, the effect isn't the same.

Just because your hero's life is in danger, or his safety is threatened, or he's going to lose his hard-earned reputation, it doesn't mean that audiences will automatically be deeply invested in what's transpiring on the page or on-screen.

If there's something else at risk besides your hero's own life, he can't walk away from a dangerous, or high-cost, situation. He must participate. Otherwise, his wife will die, or the world will end, or he'll be sent to prison for life.

But what happens if you take these stakes out of play? Then the hero is fighting the villain (or jeopardizing his job or his freedom or his reputation, etc.)…for no good reason.

If the stakes aren't strong enough, he's recklessly endangering his life or his future. He *should* walk away.

The instinct for self-preservation is strong.

At a certain point, at a subconscious (or even conscious) level, audience members are going to stop worrying about your hero's safety and start wondering why he doesn't just get the hell out of Dodge.

Once this line of thought begins, audiences will start to disengage from what they're watching or reading. Due to this emotional divestment, even the most exciting of scenes can feel dissatisfying and strangely anticlimactic.

As dynamic and thrilling as they may be externally, these scenes will feel pointless. They are melodrama and spectacle—not story.

That isn't to say that audiences will disengage completely. They don't want to see your hero die. For that matter, they don't want to see him walk away either. That isn't very heroic (although it sure is sensible).

They just might not be rooting for your hero as intensely as you intended.

In *A Few Good Men*, Daniel Kaffee must extract a confession from a powerful colonel in order to save his clients, two Guantanamo Bay marines accused of murder. Pursuing such a line of inquiry has major consequences. Kaffee could be court-martialed for professional misconduct, "Something," as the prosecuting attorney cautions, "that's gonna be stapled to every job application you [Kaffee] ever fill out."

At the climax, Kaffee goes for it. He puts Colonel Jessep on the stand. Kaffee's actively jeopardizing his career *and* his father's vaunted legacy (the cost of participation) in order to save his clients from a lifetime in prison (the stakes).

We call him a hero for it.

But if things were different, if the case were all about, let's say, fishing rights in the Bay, we'd call Kaffee a masochistic fool.

Same costs, different stakes, different effect.

I know this example is a little ridiculous. Fishing rights in Guantanamo?

Really?!

But I wanted to take it to absurd levels to drive home my point because this is one of the biggest mistakes beginners (and pros) make.

They get so caught up in their hero's dangerous exploits, they forget that his daredevilry isn't justified by the stakes. Instead of raising the tension—as these scribes intended—they've inadvertently dampened it.

In sum, if you want to keep audience involvement high, make sure that your hero is courting danger *because he's already knee-deep in trouble.*

To increase the tension, by all means, let him endanger his life or his future, but give him good cause to do so.

Give him a reason *not* to walk away.

There are two main exceptions to this. If your hero has suicidal tendencies, reckless endangerment takes on a new context, and becomes fascinating rather than alienating. If your protagonist is a child, that too, changes things. It's difficult to disengage from a child's plight, even if he was the one who put himself in harm's way.

When left *Home Alone*, Kevin does not have to protect his house from burglars. He can call the police. Even though he doesn't, even though he needlessly jeopardizes his life, audiences are still invested in his survival.

One last point of clarification: stakes of suffering are closely connected to the cost of participation, but they're not the same.

The former is a safety check of sorts. If your hero has suffered, he's encountered obstacles in pursuit of his goal, and hence, your story will contain much-needed conflict.

The cost of participation comprises the dangers associated with those obstacles. Whether these dangers are low or high cost, stakes of suffering ensure that victory isn't handed to your hero on a silver platter.

Going back to an example from *As Good As It Gets*, Melvin has to grovel in order to secure the services of a physician—a low-cost activity. In another genre, to achieve the same objective, he may have to partake in a high-speed chase, wherein death awaits at every hairpin turn—a high-cost activity.

But whether Melvin's pride or physical safety is the cost, in both cases—much to audience delight—he's definitely suffering.

The 4 Cells of the Story Stake Matrix

At this point, you may be feeling a little overwhelmed. I can understand that. You have a lot of new concepts to digest—and more are on the way.

Take heart. Your investment of time and attention will eventually pay off.

If you master the story stake matrix, you'll avoid making missteps that have vast potential to negatively affect reader experience. These mistakes are subtle and difficult to detect (especially if you're a beginner).

Correspondingly, it takes a little more effort and energy—and patience—to learn how to identify them. But once you identify these missteps, they're usually pretty easy to fix. In fact, we'll discuss specific tactics and techniques shortly.

For now, it's time to focus on the construction of the matrix itself.

The Parameters of the Story Stake Matrix

The story stake matrix has two parameters: the hierarchy of needs and the cost of participation.

Because contingency need stakes cannot, by themselves, sustain emotional involvement, they are not included in the matrix. Thus, each parameter has two variables: safety vs. spiritual needs and high vs. low costs.

If the hierarchy of needs parameter is placed on the left, and the cost of participation parameter is placed on the top, this will produce a four-celled matrix.

Starting from the bottom right and moving counterclockwise, the cells would look like this:

- low cost, spiritual needs (cell #1)
- low cost, safety needs (cell #2)
- high cost, safety needs (cell #3)
- high cost, spiritual needs (cell #4)

To help you visualize the matrix, consult the diagram below:

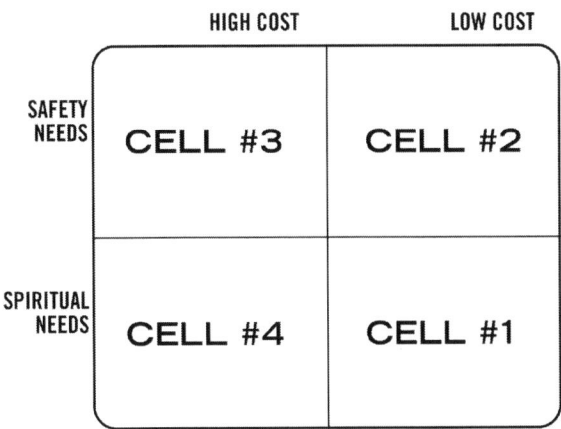

The story stake matrix.

How to Evaluate Your Story Through the Lens of the Matrix

First, you can use the matrix to assess the commercial viability of your premise. To do this, examine the stakes and modulating factors presented during Act One. If necessary, you can modify them to increase the intensity of your original concept. (We'll get into more specifics in due course.)

However, the primary function of the matrix is to evaluate the second and third acts of your story, when your hero is pursuing his goal in earnest.

Basically, you must examine the actions your hero is taking. Are they high or low cost? Then, you determine if the cost of those activities is warranted by the stakes in play.

After that, you judge how long this particular pairing will sustain audience interest before you must raise the stakes. As the result of these assessments, your story may cycle through multiple cells (usually three, at the most) or stay in the same cell throughout.

Finally, you should take stock of your climax. Which cell does your story end in? Does the combination of stakes and costs fulfill genre requirements…or not?

If your story involves multiple protagonists, you need to do evaluations from the point of view of each character. What does he have to do in a particular scene? And are the costs of those actions justified by the stakes that specifically pertain to his character?

In sum, the matrix helps you to establish and raise story stakes to create the most gripping story you can.

Now that we've laid down the groundwork for the story stake matrix, we can examine each of its cells at greater length.

Not so surprisingly, we'll start with cell #1…

- chapter four -

CELL #1: LOW COST, SPIRITUAL NEEDS

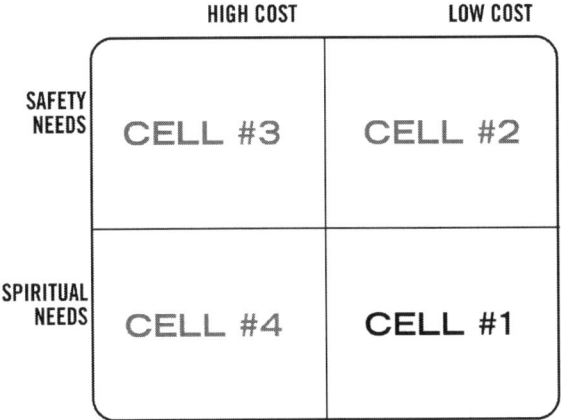

Cell #1 of the story stake matrix pairs spiritual need stakes with a low cost of participation.

I'VE DIVIDED THIS CHAPTER INTO TWO SECTIONS. ONE focuses on comedies, romances, and romantic comedies. The other focuses on action movies, thrillers, mysteries, dramas, and fantasy & science-fiction.

While there is some overlap between the tips, for the sake of simplicity, I've focused on presenting the ones that are the most pertinent to each genre.

That being said, it's still a good idea to read the tips in the action movie section even if you're planning on writing a romance (and vice versa). Actually, if you're writing a hybrid, like an action comedy or a romantic thriller, then you should definitely read the tips discussed in both sections.

Okay, let's get to it!

Comedies, Romances, and Romantic Comedies

Comedies and romantic comedies tend to start—and finish—in cell #1. The stakes begin and end with the hero's happiness. Furthermore, by definition, the costs have to remain low.

Stories in these genres are supposed to be amusing and lighthearted. It's not very funny if the protagonist has to truly risk his life, freedom, or livelihood in order to achieve his goal. Even if a protagonist does take on such risks, the tone of the story tells audiences to take the stakes as seriously as they can, but not the costs.

Romance novelists, take note: this rule about low-cost risks doesn't necessarily apply to you. I'll address this topic in more depth, later on, in chapter 5. Nonetheless, the tips in this section will still help you craft a more intriguing romance, so don't skip it!

To elicit the strongest emotional response from audiences:

(1) Spend extra time reflecting on the emotional bonding cues you plan to use.

They carry a lot of weight here, perhaps more in this cell-and-genre combination than in any other. Use as many as you can, without bogging down the pace of the beginning of your story.

(2) Emphasize the connection between the acquisition of the prize and your protagonist's self-esteem.

Just be careful not to get too heavy-handed with the details. This is a story, not a talk show!

(3) Make the prize something that your protagonist failed to gain before.

Depict the failed pursuit on-screen (like the first Santa Anita Handicap race in *Seabiscuit*), or have characters refer to it themselves. If you choose the latter, work in this backstory in a natural and dramatic way.

In a romance, the prospect of losing love will feel worse, and thus more poignant, if your protagonist has experienced this situation in the past. The greater the similarities between past and present circumstances, the stronger the effect.

To depict past hurt, you can use prologue or a flashback. Alternately, you can have the characters describe what happened through dialogue.

Hitch uses both methods to explain why both the hero and the heroine are so resistant to love. Through a flashback, audiences learn that Hitch was cruelly dumped by his college girlfriend, who was scared off by the intensity of his emotion.

Through dialogue, they learn that Sara's sister almost died in an accident. Afraid of feeling that kind of pain again, Sara limits the number of people she lets into her heart.

Be cautious with this technique.

If you get too overzealous, it can do more harm than good. Flashbacks can ruin the momentum of your story (in screenplays, especially). They can also be confusing for readers.

Additionally, dumping too much exposition about the protagonist's past pain is not appealing. Think carefully about the context of the revelation. In *Hitch*, Sara's confession carries a lot of subtext. Through it, she indicates that she is, despite her attempts not to, opening up her heart to Hitch.

As a matter of fact, the defenses of both characters are down. They are prime specimens of vulnerability. The scene is brimming with emotional intimacy, which leads me to the next tip...

(4) At the midpoint, raise the stakes by increasing your protagonists' level of commitment.

As previously discussed, if you're writing a comedy, your hero is always going to engage in low-cost activities. It doesn't matter what he does. To maintain the humor, the risks can't be taken that seriously.

Still, there are gradations between low-cost activities. After the midpoint, it's time to step it up, to have your hero really commit. It's time for him to engage in behavior that is more dangerous (superficially at least) than what he did before.

In *The Hangover*, during the first half of the second act (known in screenwriting parlance as Act 2A), the "wolf pack" can ignore the tiger in the bathroom of their hotel suite. But after the midpoint, no longer. They have to cart the beast out of the hotel and deliver it to Mike Tyson. Their cost of participation just went up, wouldn't you say?

Once the beleaguered protagonists of *Horrible Bosses* resolve to kill their employers, they try to outsource the task and hire someone else to perform the dirty deed for them. But right around the midpoint, they take on more risk, and decide to explore killing their bosses themselves.

This is a critical point. Many writers would naturally be inclined to start the second act with the protagonists trying to kill their bosses themselves. These writers would dig themselves into a hole because this position gives them little room to escalate the cost of participation. Hence, the latter half of the second act (known in screenwriting parlance as Act 2B), would likely feel boring and anticlimactic in comparison to the first half (Act 2A).

To avoid this, think carefully about what your hero has to do to achieve his goal. Have him engage in *those* actions *after* the midpoint, during Act 2B. Then, use your creative genius to brainstorm the "lite" version of these actions. This is what your hero will engage in prior to the midpoint, during Act 2A.

This method certainly won't work for every story, but if you're having problems with escalation during the second act, it could provide you with the perfect solution. (*Note*: Technically, *Horrible Bosses* starts and ends in cell #2, not cell #1. But I included it in this section because this is such an important point, and this example is easy to understand.)

In any kind of romance, the increase in commitment will, at the very least, entail some form of emotional intimacy. At the beginning of the second act, the hearts of the hero and heroine usually aren't truly engaged. Oftentimes, their interactions will have a casual, flirtatious vibe (or, if they're initially enemies, a downright hostile one).

That all changes at the midpoint.

The hero and heroine become vulnerable to one another. Through emotional intimacy alone (or emotional and physical intimacy combined), they form a true connection. If they lose each other, the negative consequences are worse than before.

If the romance ends, they won't be able to walk away, unscathed. Their hearts have become too committed for that. A breakup will cause them real heartache (which is probably one reason why they avoided intimacy in the first place).

(5) Before, or during, the climax, raise the stakes again with a sacrifice.

As a refresher, the logic goes like this: if the hero gives up something immediately prior to (or sometimes, during) the climax, failure to achieve his goal will feel worse. Now, failure not only means he lost, but also that he made his sacrifice in vain.

Little Miss Sunshine, for example, uses this concept quite creatively. Olive's brother, Dwayne, dreams about flying jets for the US Navy. But en route to Olive's beauty pageant, he makes an unpleasant discovery. He's color-blind. (You can't fly jets in the military if you're color-blind.)

Dream destroyed, Dwayne freaks out, and demands that his family pull over to the side of the road. Dwayne would like nothing more than to stay right where he is, and wallow in his misery. But he doesn't. He sacrifices his own need to grieve in order to deliver Olive to the pageant on time.

On the surface, this might not seem like much. Nevertheless, without this sacrifice, the eventual arrival of the Hoover family Volkswagen microbus at the pageant's headquarters would be far less emotionally resonant.

In romantic comedies and romances, in order to obtain love, the hero or heroine will often sacrifice their pride (or other protective mechanisms), and perhaps, in addition, a chance of career advancement.

In the case of love triangles, one (or both) of the protagonists will sacrifice a relationship with an alternate romantic prospect. There are two main ways to enhance the emotional power of this sacrifice. (*Note*: For the sake of simplicity, the following examples are illustrated from the hero's point of view, although they are equally applicable to the heroine.)

One, the alternate romantic prospect whom the hero gives up should be awesome in her own right. It's not much of a sacrifice if the hero has to choose between a subpar woman and a sublime one.

Two, because of events that have already transpired, it should appear unlikely that the heroine will forgive the hero's transgressions. When the hero initiates his final pursuit, he has little guarantee that the heroine still reciprocates his affection, and thus, incurs more of a risk.

In essence, before or at the climax, the protagonists in a romance will frequently have to sacrifice one stake for the sake of another. This works very well when the stake that gets sacrificed only involves the protagonists' personal happiness. A promotion, for instance.

In a romantic comedy, this will inevitably be the case. Again, to preserve the humor, the costs must remain low.

Things are more complicated when the protagonists must sacrifice someone else's fate for their own happiness. They can have love, but only by sacrificing their brother's own livelihood, their parents' family home, or their best friend's freedom.

These are high costs—taking us out of cell #1 altogether. Again, I will address this topic at greater length in a special section just for romance novelists. For now, it's time to venture onto the next tip.

(6) At the climax, insert a ticking clock.

Returning to *Little Miss Sunshine*, there's a reason the Hoover family doesn't arrive at Olive's beauty pageant on time, with minutes to spare. They don't have to arrive late in order to honor the essence of the characters. Nor do they have to arrive late to honor the rules of that particular story world.

This is a deliberate restriction—artificially imposed by the writer—in order to increase the urgency, and hence, the tension during the climax.

To give your audience the most intense emotional experience, follow *Sunshine*'s model. Don't give your protagonist a second to spare.

In fact, *Sunshine* goes the extra mile and gives audiences not one, but two (!) ticking clocks. In addition to the clock immediately prior to the pageant, there's one included within the pageant itself.

Backstage, an aide keeps pressuring Olive to take the platform for the talent portion of the competition. Again, the aide doesn't have to rush Olive for the sake of authenticity. Few movie-goers would be familiar with pageant timetables.

This is a case of exploiting naturally occurring elements of the setting in order to maximize the urgency of the scene. If you look hard enough at the setting of your climax, you should be able to do the same.

Action Movies, Thrillers, Mysteries, Dramas, and Fantasy & Science-Fiction

In contrast to comedies and romantic comedies, the bulk of action movies, thrillers, mysteries, dramas, and fantasy & science-fiction stories neither begin nor end in cell #1.

Sleuth-based stories are a major exception to this rule. By sleuth-based, I'm talking about stories where the goal of the protagonist (whether an amateur or a professional) is to solve a case that originates with a dead body.

At first, the sleuth must catch the perpetrator for the sake of justice (spiritual need stakes). Plus, his investigation will initially require low-cost participation, like collecting evidence or interviewing witnesses.

The combination of spiritual needs and low costs places these stories squarely in cell #1. To enhance the commercial appeal of such stories, consider the following:

(1) Link the sleuth's backstory to (a) the victim, (b) a prime suspect, or (c) another investigator.

Your story will inherently be more interesting when there's a personal connection between the two parties, even if it's tenuous and remote.

For instance, in *Lethal Weapon*, Murtaugh served in the military with the victim's father. Murtaugh hasn't spoken to the man in years, but their shared past adds intrigue to the story's beginning.

The closer the connection, however, the more effective the tactic.

A case where the victim is a mentor who supported the sleuth during tough times is going to be more powerful than a case where the victim is a colleague from another department whom the sleuth barely knows.

(2) Forge a connection between the victim and audiences.

Begin your story by introducing the victim before he is killed. Use emotional bonding cues to make him likeable, sympathetic, or fascinating.

This method comes with two warnings: one, audiences can potentially feel cheated.

That is to say, they invest their emotions into a character…only to discover, a few pages later, that this character has been basically removed from the story altogether—rendering their emotional investment, to some degree, a waste. On the other hand, this situation can also intensify their desire to see the hero obtain justice on behalf of the victim.

Second, it's also possible that audiences can connect so strongly with the victim, that their emotional identification with your sleuth might be weak by the time you get around to introducing him.

To avoid the second pitfall, you could introduce your sleuth first, cementing the bond between him and audiences, and then in a following scene, have him meet the victim (before, obviously, the victim is killed). Thus, audiences still get to know the victim, *but through the point of view of your hero.*

(3) Couple stakes of reputation with setting.

While the murder remains unsolved, a dark cloud will hang over someone's good name, possibly jeopardizing this person's chances of political or social advancement.

(4) Add in stakes of happiness.

Make it known that the sleuth's own career advancement hinges upon solving the case.

If he fails to bring it to a successful conclusion, he won't lose his job (that would shift your story into cell #2), but his prospects of a promotion or a better job elsewhere will be destroyed.

This technique is particularly effective if you are exploring a theme of ambition in your story.

(5) Include a deadline from the outset.

Giving the sleuth a limited time frame to solve the case does not create the same degree of tension as a ticking clock, but it still helps. (Incidentally, you might incorporate a ticking clock later on, after you've raised the stakes.)

The General's Daughter, for example, uses almost all of these techniques to get audiences involved in the mystery of who killed the eponymous victim.

Paul, a military investigative agent, has two interactions with the victim before she is killed. These interactions make him (and audiences) more invested in finding her killer than if they hadn't gotten to know her prior to her untimely death.

Actually, Paul's connection to her runs deeper than that. Paul served under the general in Vietnam, and it's hinted that this case will test Paul's loyalty to him.

Additionally, Paul is given a mere 36 hours to solve the case before the FBI descends and turns everything into a media frenzy. Under normal circumstances, this would hardly be ideal. Because the general is a serious contender for vice president, in this situation, a media frenzy has even more serious repercussions.

Finally, Paul is assigned a partner to help him solve the case. A woman. And not just any woman, either. In the past, he had an affair with her when she was engaged to someone else!

Raising the Stakes and Shifting into Cell #2

Even with the enhancements described above, your story cannot remain in cell #1 forever. By or at the midpoint, you need to raise the stakes and transition into cell #2 (or, in some rare cases, possibly cell #4).

In a nutshell, to accomplish this, modify circumstances so that, in addition to spiritual need stakes, your protagonist is driven by safety need stakes: general protection, demise, livelihood, freedom, sanity, reputation, or access. (Be careful with the last two. Remember they can be classified as either spiritual or safety need stakes; it depends on context.)

To see how doing this can work to your advantage, let's revisit *White Collar*. This example has several nuances, though, so bear with me. In episode five from season four, "Honor Among Thieves," Neal wants a crime scene report that will hopefully, among other things, help him figure out who murdered his surrogate mother (stakes of justice).

Trouble is, the report is stored in a database server located on the 22nd floor of the federal marshal building. Although Neal's a talented thief, Neal's tracking anklet (ironically monitored by the federal marshals) prevents him from stealing the file himself. Plus, Peter, Neal's FBI handler—and more important, friend—would easily deduce Neal's involvement.

A female thief tempts Neal with a deal: steal a pricey work of art for her, and she'll steal the police file for him. Neal refuses because, for him, the cost—Peter's trust—is too great. Although it's too high for Neal, notice that according to our definitions, this cost of participation is low. (There's another—more serious—cost involved, but for the sake of illustration, we're only going to focus on this one.)

Despite Neal's refusal, the female thief doesn't let it go. She reveals to Neal that she broke in anyway and stole (technically, I suppose, copied) the file. And when she did, she planted strands of Neal's hair at the scene of the crime.

If Neal doesn't steal the artwork for her, she'll tell the marshals that he broke into their building. Even though he didn't, with all the evidence pointing his way, he'll go to jail for sure.

Voila, there it is! The stakes have been raised. They have gone from justice (spiritual needs, cell #1) to freedom (safety needs, cell #2).

Notice the effect of raising the stakes. They're now so high, they override Neal's initial reluctance to betray Peter. This is an important point because Peter has put his career on the line—more than once—to save Neal, who should repay Peter with his loyalty.

Still, because safety need stakes are involved, audiences can understand and support Neal's decision. Critically, in spite of his betrayal, Neal's likeability is preserved—yet another example of how powerful story stakes can be when they are employed with skill.

That's not all. Neal doesn't seem like he's backtracking just so the episode can conveniently go where it was headed all along (the artwork heist). His decision to reverse course is completely believable, nipping potential complaints in the bud. Rather than grumble about contrivance, audiences are free to fully enjoy the hijinks of the heist.

Although this episode of *White Collar* manages it quite nicely, sustaining audience involvement until you raise the stakes and shift into cell #2 from cell #1 is kind of an uphill battle. Frankly, even with the techniques described in this chapter (such as linking the sleuth's backstory to another party), it requires tremendous skill to pull off with success.

If you're not a master of dialogue, suspense, or—if you're writing a buddy cop mystery—humor, you're probably better off beginning with more of a bang, i.e. with cell #2.

Put another stake into play—specifically a safety need stake—during Act One. Because it grabs reader interest right away, this addition will make your concept "an easier sell."

For instance:

Stakes of Justice + Stakes of Livelihood

Your sleuth botched up his last case so bad, his boss is at the end of his rope. If your sleuth doesn't seal this case up and deliver an answer wrapped in a red ribbon, he can kiss his job good-bye.

Stakes of Justice + Stakes of General Protection

There's more than just one dead body. All evidence points to a serial killer. If the sleuth doesn't solve the case soon, more innocent people will die.

Stakes of Justice + A Hint of Stakes of Demise

The perpetrator of the crime knows that the sleuth has been assigned to the perpetrator's case. To scare off the sleuth, the perpetrator calls the sleuth and threatens to harm him or his family if the sleuth persists in his investigation.

The sleuth reckons that if he catches the perpetrator, the sleuth will not only achieve justice but also prevent the perp from ever coming after his family.

You can also use this tactic to create a misleading clue, or red herring. That is, the perpetrator of the crime doesn't threaten the sleuth. It just looks that way.

The person really making the threat didn't kill the victim, but this person is, nevertheless, afraid of what secrets the sleuth's investigation might uncover, and so, tries to use coercion to stop it.

Stakes of Justice + Stakes of Freedom + Stakes of Access

Evidence leads to one prime suspect: a father with three children. Still, despite it, the sleuth feels that the suspect is innocent. If the sleuth doesn't exonerate him in time, the suspect will go to jail, and the suspect's kids will become wards of the state.

By starting your story in cell #2, notice that you'll no longer be able to raise the stakes by shifting from cell #1 to cell #2 at the midpoint. How then, do you raise the stakes? We'll discuss various methods at the end of chapter 5. For now, let's tackle—

A Major Exception: Classic Whodunits and Cozy Mysteries

Classic whodunits and cozy mysteries may squarely begin and end here, in cell #1.

The likeability of the sleuth, the appeal of the setting, and curiosity over who did it—and why—keep readers turning the pages.

This holds true, even if the sleuth's activities are limited to gossip and observation, which carry little, if any, risk.

Gosford Park is one such example. The story contains no danger to anyone (save the victim). As a matter of fact, 80 minutes pass before he's even murdered! And when an amateur sleuth of sorts, a young Scottish maid, confronts two perpetrators, she does so without any risk to her safety.

Although excitement isn't provided through thrilling high-cost activities, the film is not without its charms. Audience interest is sustained through other means, mainly: anticipation of the murder itself, curiosity over who actually did it, and fascination with the class divide between the suspects.

- chapter five -

CELL #2: LOW COST, SAFETY NEEDS

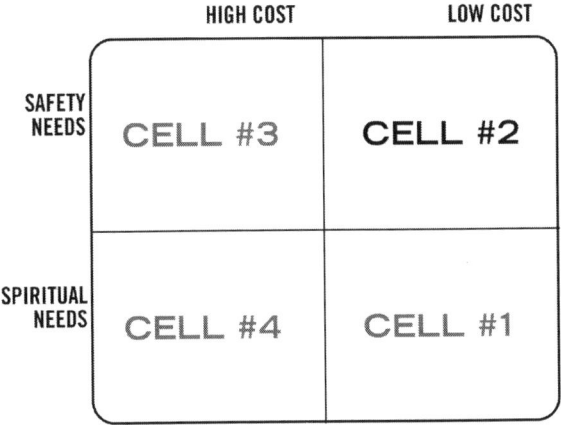

Cell #2 of the story stake matrix pairs safety need stakes with a low cost of participation.

BASED ON GENRE, THIS CHAPTER IS DIVIDED INTO three sections:

- comedies and romantic comedies
- romances, specifically romance novels
- action movies, etc.

Note: If you're writing a romantic comedy screenplay, the tips in the romance novel section may still be helpful to you. All the same, please realize that they are primarily intended for novelists. (The hypothetical premise, especially, isn't high-concept enough for a feature film.)

Comedies and Romantic Comedies

It's rare for a comedy or romantic comedy to start or finish in cell #2. If yours does, first, let me advise you to follow the same pointers as for cell #1.

Second, let me offer my congratulations! Safety needs tend to evoke a stronger degree of emotion than spiritual needs. Thus, you have an extra advantage over your competition.

Groundhog Day, *Mrs. Doubtfire*, *Legally Blonde*, and *Liar Liar* were megahits. Sure, they all are high concept and well executed. But it's their stakes that truly elevate them. If the protagonist fails at the end, he risks more than just unhappiness.

In the case of the former two, safety needs (freedom and access to children, respectively) are at stake from the very beginning. In the case of the latter two, freedom and access to children, respectively, are also at stake. However, these stories begin in cell #1 and transition into cell #2 around the midpoint or immediately prior to the climax.

To be clear, you can write a great comedy or romantic comedy without transitioning your story into cell #2. But if you're feeling ambitious and want to give yourself a writing challenge, find ways for your story stakes to encompass more than just your hero's own happiness.

Brainstorming along these lines could greatly enhance the blockbuster potential of your original comedic concept!

A Special Note for Romance Novelists

A lot of tips and examples in this book focus on other genres. At this time, I want to take a moment to focus specifically on a hypothetical that will help you, the aspiring romance novelist. If you have no interest in writing a romance novel, you might want to skip ahead to the next section.

Unlike romantic comedies, which need to maintain a lighthearted tone, romance novels routinely incorporate safety need stakes into their plots. For example, one protagonist may try to preserve his (or her) freedom or livelihood through low-cost activities. Typically, these entail romancing the other protagonist under false pretenses.

Furthermore, protagonists can sometimes make high-cost sacrifices in order to gain love. For instance, if the heroine marries the hero, she will lose access to her parents.

While these situations technically can be described with the story stake matrix, in this circumstance, using the lens of the matrix may be more trouble than it's worth.

So, we will abandon it for now. Instead, we will distill the principles behind it to two core issues: (1) how to use stakes to enhance your initial premise, and (2) what to do when your hero or heroine has to make a high-cost sacrifice for love.

Note: If you're writing a romantic thriller, the tips in this section won't necessarily apply. The tips discussed in the action movie section in this chapter, however, will. Please be sure to read it (along with chapter 6, which covers cell #3)!

How to Use Stakes to Enhance the Initial Premise of Your Romance Novel

In our hypothetical example, the hero and heroine are both landscape architects. In fact, they are competing over a lucrative waterfront development contract to be awarded by the city. To spice things up a little, we'll throw in a "false pretenses" gambit.

The hero, for whatever reason, doesn't have enough time to design his own architectural plans. Instead, he intends to woo the heroine to get a peek at her own designs, copy the best ideas, and perhaps, undercut her proposed budget.

This is our basic premise. It's got lots of potential for personal and professional conflict. But it's not complete because it lacks stakes.

We have the *what*—the contract—but what about the *why*?

Why is securing this contract so important to the protagonists?

We'll start with the heroine. She's just started her own architecture firm. As owner of a fledgling operation, she needs to quickly establish her professional reputation. Getting the contract will secure her future. Failing to get it would ruin her entrepreneurial dreams.

This is a fine start, but it's a little too "me-oriented" for my liking. To soften it up, we could try this: she started her firm against the advice of her family, who told her it would be too risky, and that 80%–90% of small businesses fail within their first few years of operation.

While that might work, in this example, we're going to take another tack. Her financial success is going to affect more than her own level of happiness. It's going to affect the life of someone else precious to her…like a younger sister…in, let's say, moderate trouble.

This sibling is constantly being teased by her female classmates. It's not full-scale bullying—not yet—but the heroine is afraid it's going to reach that point soon. If the heroine gets the waterfront contract, she'll have enough funds to send her sister to a private school, far, far away from the bullying crowd.

See the difference the stakes make? If readers weren't rooting for the heroine before, they'd really be rooting for her now.

To get them even more invested, let's play around with the heroine's backstory. Up until recently, she was working at a much larger company. Before she left, she had been up for a promotion.

She probably would've gotten it too, but a relationship with one of her coworkers distracted her.

She was so consumed by their romance, she let her work slip. Not a lot, but enough so that she didn't look like the best candidate for the promotion. The man she had been dating got it instead.

Actually, he had wooed her purposefully so she'd lose focus. After he secured the promotion, he immediately broke off their relationship. Every time she saw him in the hallways or at staff meetings, the heroine was reminded of her stupidity. She couldn't take it anymore, so she left. *That* was the impetus for her to start her own firm.

This addition enhances our story in multiple ways:

- It gives the heroine a strong reason to resist the hero's overtures, besides the fact that we need their conflict to keep the plot going!
- When the heroine discovers the truth about the hero, the similarity of it to her past experience makes this current emotional blow even more devastating for her—and more compelling for audiences.
- Finally, if the hero learns about the heroine's past (and meets her little sister), it will be harder for him to suppress the twinges of his conscience, generating a healthy dose of internal conflict.

Speaking of the hero, he's coming across as a rather unsavory fellow, isn't he? At this stage, he doesn't seem worthy of the heroine's affections or reader empathy…but he might be—if we add some stakes to the picture.

As a starting point, let's say that he's driven by ambition. If he can bring in the lucrative waterfront contract, he'll be promoted to a member of the board of the midsized firm where he works.

While this gives him a credible motivation, because he has to seduce the heroine, his motives need to be less mercenary. By the end, of course, he will fall in love with her, and likely abandon his scheme.

But, readers still have to care about him before he views the heroine as more than just a mark. Otherwise, they won't be that happy about the "happily ever after," when the hero and heroine are finally united in love.

So what can we do? We must raise the stakes.

Let's try this: the midsized firm where the hero works was founded by his great-great-great-grandfather (or someone like that). It's been run by the oldest son in each generation for over a century.

But now, it's fallen on tough times. If the company doesn't get a major cash infusion soon, it'll have to be sold to an out-of-state corporation that wants to use the family firm's illustrious pedigree for its own (probably no-good) purposes.

The hero and his dad have always had a strained relationship. In fact, the hero uses his mother's maiden name to distance himself from his father and his father's dreams for the hero's future. (The name issue will also enable the hero to befriend the heroine without making her look stupid for not realizing that he's working for the competition.)

Maybe, to avoid the responsibilities he feels his dad is forcing upon him, the hero has spent the last 5 years abroad, dilly-dallying in Europe. When he returns home, he discovers that his dad is dying, that the family firm is in trouble, and that his dreams are more in alignment with his dad's than he ever realized.

The dad, on his deathbed, asks his son to maintain the family legacy and protect the firm from the circling corporate sharks. The hero solemnly promises to do so.

Good stuff, good stuff. Right?

But we still have a problem: the hero should rely on his own merit, rather than trying to steal design ideas from the heroine. This is another truth that requires softening. Perhaps, the hero's own guilt and grief are preventing him from developing suitably grand ideas of his own.

There might be a time crunch too, and the hero doesn't feel he has enough time to design something good. Maybe he's always been inclined to take the easy way out—that could have been a source of contention between him and his dad—so instead of relying on his degree in architecture to get ahead, he decides to rely on his degree in seduction.

We're getting there, definitely getting there.

Depending on what we do with scenes told from the hero's point of view, I think audiences will sympathize with him. They still won't want him to succeed with his scheme. All the same, it's enough so that they won't be completely alienated by his behavior till he changes course.

Let's say though, that writing the hero's interior monologue is proving to be more difficult than expected. Is there another way we can get audiences onboard?

Why yes, yes there is.

We can raise the stakes yet again, so that they encompass more than just the family legacy.

For instance, a husband-and-wife team could've worked at the hero's firm for years. While industrious, they're not particularly imaginative, so they can't contribute to designing the waterfront project (in case you were wondering).

But, they have provided the hero with something far better. Lacking children of their own, they have treated him like their own son. As a child, the hero often sought out the husband for advice rather than his own dad.

If the out-of-state corporation buys the hero's firm, the hero knows that the couple will be fired, and their pensions probably destroyed. To protect these people, the hero will do anything to stop the takeover—including taking advantage of the heroine.

We've got a solid combination, now, don't we? Can you see the plot unfolding naturally from these basic elements?

And, furthermore, can you see how readers would invest more in the protagonists' journey than if the hero and heroine were after the waterfront contract only for personal gain?

When Your Hero or Heroine Must Make High-Cost Sacrifices

As we both know, at the end of our hypothetical story, the hero and heroine are going to be united in love. To get there, at least one of them will have to make a sacrifice.

Because the hero is the one approaching the heroine under false pretenses, it stands to reason that he should be the one to give something up. In basic terms, we can think of it like this: he has to sacrifice Stake A (whatever motivated him to pursue the waterfront contract) in order to achieve Stake B (personal happiness generated by his relationship with the heroine).

Sounds simple, right?

Don't be deceived. It's a danger zone loaded with potential problems.

See, once the hero decides to sacrifice Stake A, it's no longer a stake. It transforms into a cost—the price he must pay in order to achieve Stake B.

If this cost only affects his personal happiness, you're golden. The hero can give up his personal ambition for love—and with full support of your audience. Likewise, he can give up the family legacy (assuming no other siblings are involved) without incurring reader wrath. These are both low costs.

Things get trickier when the costs run higher.

If the hero sacrifices the livelihood of the husband and wife who treated him like their own son, he's not noble. He's selfish. He's no longer worthy of the heroine's love, nor your reader's affection.

Whatever you do, don't drop the husband-and-wife stakes because they've suddenly become troublesome. They can't miraculously evaporate from your story. (I've seen this happen more than once!)

Additionally, the hero can't come to the realization that the couple would want him to choose love over their own well-being. At least, he can't make that realization all on his own. If that were the case, what prevented him from making this realization earlier on?

Nothing, nothing but your need to keep the hero and heroine apart.

Savvy readers will immediately recognize this contrivance. When your hero finally goes after the heroine, they won't be cheering him on. They'll be musing on how convenient it is for him to come to this remarkable realization…just as your story is coming to a close.

Instead, try one of these options:

(1) Remove the stakes from your story altogether.

This is perhaps the simplest solution. Don't use stakes that are linked to other characters at all.

Stick to stakes that affect only the hero's own happiness.

On one hand, this solves the problem. On the other, it has the potential to significantly decrease the amount of tension permeating your story, making for a less satisfying read.

If you think the tradeoff is worth it, then go for it. If not, try one of the other options below.

(2) Take the stakes out of play.

Instead of removing these stakes from your story, keep them in. But, when appropriate, take them out of play. Here's how:

In this situation, someone's future hangs in the balance. Whoever that is, that person needs to have a conversation with the hero and give the hero his blessing to proceed. (This, you'll note, is a lot different than having the hero *give himself* permission to sacrifice another person's future for the sake of his own.)

The hero's still paying a high cost, but this way, he doesn't seem selfish for doing so. The "collateral damage" aspect has been eliminated. Hence, readers can fully invest in the hero's decision as well as his final pursuit of the heroine.

(3) Have the hero choose the other set of stakes over love.

In this option, the hero knows that his decision will preclude a romantic relationship with the heroine. But the costs are too high for him not to sacrifice his own happiness.

However, although the heroine has been betrayed, she acknowledges the difficulty of the hero's situation. Contrary to his expectations, she magnanimously forgives him. He, happily, promises to spend the rest of his life making it up to her.

(4) Find a way for the hero to have his cake and eat it too.

Basically, you must use your ingenuity so that the hero doesn't have to make a sacrifice at all.

Somehow, he finds a way to preserve someone else's future, while, at the same time, ensuring his own happiness.

If you're not careful, though, this tactic may seem very contrived. You can't pull your happy ending out of a magic hat.

In our hypothetical, the hero can't suddenly receive a windfall, which would give him the cash he needs to forestall the takeover of the family firm, thus putting an end to his competition with the heroine.

Well…he can't receive that windfall out of the blue.

If you weave in hints about your magical solution, it's a different matter altogether. Stock options, mysterious benefactors, royal relatives—all can extricate your hero—as long as you set them up beforehand.

Action Movies, etc.

As with comedies, romances, and romantic comedies, action movies, thrillers, mysteries, dramas, and fantasy & science-fiction stories that begin with safety needs at stake are able to conjure a greater depth of emotion than those that begin with spiritual needs.

Start your story in cell #2, and you start from a position of strength.

Remember, emotion is the key standard by which your story will be judged. If yours can elicit a deeper emotional investment from audiences, captivating them from its very beginning, you've substantially increased the commercial viability of your concept.

Because you're starting from a stronger foundation, observe that the effect of modulating factors is multiplied. It's like multiplying 100 by 5 versus multiplying 10 by 5.

Take deadlines, for instance. Which is more suspenseful: having 48 hours to discover who killed a victim (stakes of justice, cell #1) or having 48 hours to rescue a missing person *before* he is killed (stakes of general protection, cell #2)?

Once you've hooked audiences with your high-stake premise, you need to sustain and, hopefully, deepen their involvement.

To achieve this, consider using the following three-pronged approach:

(1) During the first act, employ the same techniques as suggested for sleuth-based stories that begin their second act in cell #1.

To quickly recap, these include:

- creating hero backstory that connects him to present-day characters
- developing the audience-stake bond
- coupling stakes of reputation with a high-stake setting
- adding in stakes of happiness (specifically a job promotion)
- including a deadline from the outset

To these, you can add another modulator—using children (or childlike adults) as story stakes.

Technically, this modulator could be used in cell #1. The murder of a child is automatically going to elicit more emotion than the murder of an adult. However, I find it rather macabre to make this suggestion.

It's more palatable for me to recommend that you use children as story stakes with the knowledge that while their young lives are at stake at the beginning, these lives will be saved by the end.

To understand how modulating factors can deepen audience involvement, even when you start with a high-stake, "cell #2" premise, let us once again examine *Taken*.

Bryan Mills's daughter, Kimmy, is abducted by a prostitution ring (stakes of demise). How can this situation be any worse? How can audiences become more invested in the outcome than they already are? Is it even possible?

Indeed, it is.

First of all, Bryan only has 96 hours to rescue Kimmy before it'll become impossible to track her whereabouts.

As discussed previously, due to the demands of his job, Bryan has neglected his relationship with Kimmy in the past. If he doesn't save her now, he will never be able to make amends (stakes of regret).

During the first act, audiences spend a decent amount of time with Kimmy. Because they know she has a passion for horses and has dreamed about becoming a singer since she was 5 years old, their bond with her is strong. (Although we're focusing on the groundwork laid down during Act One, it should be mentioned that this bond is reinforced throughout Act Two through several reminders.)

Kimmy is no longer a child; she's on the cusp of adulthood. Nevertheless, her innocence is preserved in one key respect. Unlike the friend who was abducted the same time she was, Kimmy is still a virgin. It's a terrible thing to be abducted and then forced into the sex trade. But if this is Kimmy's first experience, her nightmare becomes even more nightmarish.

Together, all of these details make Kimmy's dire predicament—which is intense and emotionally compelling to begin with—even *more* intense and compelling.

This is the mark of a pro.

Amateurs would be content to have devised a high-stake premise: a CIA-trained operative goes to Paris to save his daughter.

Boom! They think they're set.

Pros, on the other hand, know better. To rise above the competition, they can't skate by on stakes alone. Through skillful use of modulating factors, they go beyond that, pushing audiences to the emotional edge—from the story's very beginning.

That's not all. This use of modulating factors will have positive consequences (in terms of storytelling), which will reverberate throughout the story.

Imagine, for a second, if these modulating factors were removed from the beginning of *Taken*. Bryan has a good relationship with Kimmy; he isn't trying to make amends. Audiences are never shown Kimmy's passion for horses or music. Kimmy isn't a virgin.

Then, think about some of the actions that Bryan has to take during the second act: investigating the apartment from where Kimmy was taken, hiring a nervous translator, evading local police, single-handedly destroying a construction site, watching Kimmy being auctioned off to the highest bidder.

Think about the climax and resolution too: chasing (either by foot or via Audi) the fancy boat where Kimmy has been transported, leaping onto the vessel, killing every bad guy onboard. Kimmy, hugging her dad, telling him "I love you," (and, unlike earlier, not because she's emotionally blackmailing him to secure his parental consent for her trip).

Without the Act One details listed above, do you think audience response would be the same to Acts Two and Three?

Nope. Me, neither.

Whether Bryan's participating in low- or high-cost activities to rescue his daughter, these actions are going to elicit a deeper degree of emotion based on what transpired during Act One.

A pro writer uses this knowledge to his advantage. Accordingly, he adjusts his first act so that an objectively high-stake situation subjectively feels "higher." I encourage you to do the same.

(2) Increase the cost of participation and shift your story into cell #3.

Due to the high stakes already in play, undercurrents of tension will permeate the first half of Act Two.

These currents help sustain audience involvement, even when your protagonist is engaged in common low-cost activities such as interviewing witnesses, assembling a team, or training for his mission.

But your story can't stay in cell #2 forever. At some point, your hero needs to risk more than embarrassment, humiliation, the loss of a promotion or legacy, or simply wasted time and other resources.

He has to put some skin in the game.

If participation in his journey doesn't cost your hero something major, you will either relegate your story to the ghetto of mediocrity or fail completely to make good on the promises implied by your genre—or both.

Plus, when you stick to low-cost activities, audiences are not going to stew about your hero's safety.

Why should they, when he's not doing anything that dangerous?

You're missing out on a prime opportunity to amplify their tension, and correspondingly, keep them turning the pages of your story.

So, when's a good time to increase the cost of participation?

The answer is the same as in comedies, romances, and romantic comedies: the midpoint.

The midpoint is when several stories increase the hero's cost of participation and make the transition from cell #2 to cell #3. The longer you delay, the more you risk audience disengagement before you get to the juicy stuff.

In fact, many writers view the midpoint as a "point of no return" for the hero. During Act 2A, he may've had options on the table. But around the midpoint, the costs increase, the stakes are raised, and those options vanish for good.

There are no more remaining exits; they've all been sealed off. It's time for your protagonist to fully commit to his journey.

At first, *Thelma and Louise* can preserve their freedom through low-cost activities: driving, arguing, renting motel rooms, and engaging in romantic liaisons. Eventually, though, to keep audiences invested, the two women will have to take on more risks during Act 2B, and fully commit to being outlaws.

To get much-needed cash, Thelma robs a grocery store. To avoid being arrested, both ladies lock a police officer inside the trunk of his own cruiser. These actions are not only dangerous, they carry severe penalties.

Before, there was a possibility, a small one, but still a possibility that Thelma and Louise could, if they wanted, return to their old lives. But once Thelma's robbery is caught on tape, that option ceases to exist.

To quote the detective tracking them, "There's two girls out there that had a chance. They *had* a chance…now, they're in serious trouble."

Raising Costs Prior to the Midpoint

Many action movies and thrillers will actually increase the hero's cost of participation sooner, about halfway through Act 2A.

In *Taken*, this happens when Bryan pursues the spotter who gave the prostitution ring his daughter's address (as well as when he beats up the spotter's accomplice).

We can find the same pattern in *Inception*. Costs rise the first time when Cobb teaches Ariadne the basics of lucid dreaming. When she gets nervous, objects around them start to explode. Within the same sequence, Ariadne will be stabbed by Cobb's wife.

Costs rise again later on in Act 2A, when Cobb ventures to Mombasa to recruit a forger to his inception team. Unlike hiring Ariadne, recruiting this forger is much more dangerous. That's because Mombasa happens to be "the backyard" for a shady corporation that has a price on Cobb's head. Once discovered by its agents, Cobb must run for his life in a thrilling chase sequence.

Although these 2A scenes fulfill genre requirements, they're usually not terribly risky. Or, if they are risky, they're brief or small in scope. I think of them as "action-lite," or in the case of *Inception*, as "pseudo-thrills."

Ariadne, you'll notice, is not in any real danger. She's dreaming. Cobb's wife can't really hurt her. But it doesn't feel that way to Ariadne—nor to audience members who are experiencing the story from Ariadne's point of view.

These kinds of Act 2A scenes, with action-lite and pseudo-thrills, are quite beneficial. Why? They help sustain audience investment, but still give you enough room to escalate the tension and, through a more extensive set of stunts or thrills, raise the costs (and hence the stakes) at the midpoint.

If you've already significantly delivered on the genre goods during, or at the very tail end of, Act One, you might not need to incorporate an action-lite sequence before you reach the midpoint.

That being said, the best stories tend to fulfill genre requirements as often as possible—while being cognizant of other factors, such as—

Pacing

Your entire second act can't be an action stunt. Audiences will soon tire of your hero's exploits and become just as bored as if there were no action at all. Once you transition from cell #2 into cell #3, per the dictates of pacing, you should (as illustrated in the diagram below), oscillate between the two. Your hero will have to resume low-cost activities just to give audiences a respite from the action or thrills:

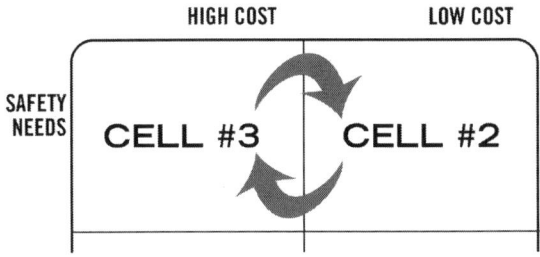

To avoid tiring out audiences, your protagonist must periodically resume low-cost activities.

To sustain audience engagement without wearying them out—and without reverting your story back to cell #2—consider increasing the cost of participation *without* actively endangering your hero's physical life.

For example, if your protagonist pursues his path of inquiry, he risks losing his job—not a promotion—but his very means of livelihood. (We've seen this already in *A Few Good Men*.)

This type of risk creates something I like to call "the hover effect." Knowledge of it is always there, hovering at the back of audiences' minds, coloring their experience of what's unfolding on-screen or on the page.

Even when your hero is engaged in objectively low-cost activities, because high-cost danger constantly lurks in the background, these scenes will subjectively feel more tense. By marrying high costs with slow pacing, you get the best of both worlds. It's a win-win all around.

There's another option too. It's the last element of our three-pronged approach:

(3) Add new stakes to those already in play.

If you want audiences to care even more about what happens to your hero, then…give them more to care about.

Unfortunately, adding a new set of story stakes (ideally one that concerns safety needs) at the midpoint, or sometime thereafter, is easier said than done. Hopefully, the collection of examples below will inspire you during your own plotting sessions.

Making Things Worse

Sometimes, adding new stakes is a matter of sheer brainstorming, of persistently asking yourself if there's a way to make things worse for your hero. You might have to play around with the rules of your story world to accomplish this.

To illustrate, let's return to *Inception*. Around the midpoint, Cobb and his crew descend into the first dream level. There, they discover that their target, Fischer, has militarized his subconscious. Contrary to their expectations, the protagonists will have to deal with automatic rifles and a freight train.

The film already established that if you're killed in a dream, you'll just wake up. That low-cost penalty is fine for the beginning of the second act. But not here, not now. If venturing into various dream levels carries no danger, then all the action with the guns and the train is pointless.

The premise, as intriguing as it is, becomes boring.

Knowing this, writer and director Christopher Nolan increased the costs, permanently shifting the story into cell #3. Due to the potency of the sedative the team had to take to descend into three dream levels, if they're killed on any of the levels, they won't wake up.

Instead, they'll be sent to Limbo: raw, infinite subconscious with nothing in it except for whatever was left behind by someone who's been trapped there before. If left there, they will likely forget all about the real world. And even if they do remember its existence, by the time they figure it out and return, their minds probably will've been turned into mush.

As Cobb says, "Downwards is the only way forwards." To exit the dream levels and return to the real world, his crew will have to descend deeper and deeper into this alternate reality—where they will encounter Fischer's heavily-armed subconscious projections at every turn (who, again, by fatally wounding Cobb and his crew, will send them to Limbo).

In other words, the protagonists must *risk* their sanity in order to *preserve* it.

Nifty little trick, isn't it?

Although ingenious, adding stakes of sanity, on top of the stakes of access already present, is not that intuitive (which is why I said that you might have to play around with the rules of your story world to add a new set of stakes to your story).

Incidentally, observe that the stakes of access in *Inception* are overlaid by stakes of regret. Cobb's separation from his children puts him in a desperate position indeed; but his guilt over not calling out their names and seeing their faces one last time—when he had the chance to do so—makes his situation even more poignant.

Because it relies on the time-tested trope of time travel, our next example of putting new stakes into play is a little more straightforward than *Inception*'s. At first, in *Back to the Future*, when Marty McFly ventures back to the year 1955, the negative consequences are bad—but not that bad. He's trapped in a different time period, without his girlfriend.

As far as stakes of freedom go, these are pretty low-key. Marty may be unhappy about the situation, but hey, he's not behind bars! He's still got free will. He's still alive.

That possibility, however, changes—you guessed it—right around the midpoint. When Marty shows Doc a photo of Marty's family, it's revealed that Marty's brother has been partially erased from the picture. As Doc concludes, if Marty doesn't find a way to get his parents to fall in love, Marty will cease to exist.

Cha-ching!

The stakes just got higher.

As a side note, notice that later on, at the Enchantment Under the Sea dance, the photo takes on extra functionality. First, it *reminds* audiences that Marty will die, should he fail to reunite his parents at the dance.

At the same time, it acts as a *ticking clock*: Marty must get his parents to share their first kiss before he completely vanishes from the picture. Study this example carefully. It exemplifies the kind of economy that all storytellers should aspire to.

In both *Inception* and *Back to the Future*, the stakes were raised by adding another set of safety need stakes on top of the safety need stakes already present. This task may seem impossible to you.

Don't sweat it. I started with the hard stuff first. There is an easier way to raise the stakes, that old standby—

Making Things Personal

If you start with general stakes of protection, there are different ways to make things personal for your hero, and thus, raise the stakes. Here are two:

In *Sherlock Holmes: A Game of Shadows*, Holmes is trying to stop the diabolical Professor Moriarty from embroiling Europe in war. When the professor explicitly refuses to "take Watson out of the equation," things turn personal for Holmes.

The detective must jeopardize his own life and stop Moriarty not just to avert a world war (general stakes), but also to save the life of his best friend (stakes of demise).

Frank Farmer is hired to be *The Bodyguard* to superstar Rachel Marron because a stalker has been sending her threatening letters. At the film's outset, saving her life is just a job to Frank. She represents general stakes that he's been assigned to protect.

But around the midpoint, after he and Rachel enjoy a date that's both sexy and romantic, the stakes undergo a fundamental alteration. If he fails to save her, it won't just hurt him professionally; it will hurt him personally too. Rachel's character has shifted from representing general stakes of protection to stakes of demise.

Complicating matters further, a romantic entanglement clouds Frank's judgment, making it even more likely he will fail—which is why he quickly extinguishes their affair, incurring her wrath and generating more sparks and more conflict!

• • •

It is possible to craft a gripping second act without raising the cost of participation or adding in new stakes. Take *The Silence of the Lambs*. Despite the use of modulating factors, the stakes—although high—essentially remain the same, while Clarice's participation stays low.

Sure, she has to deal with a cannibalistic serial killer. But although Hannibal Lecter is sadistically clever, he's confined during all their interactions. Clarice doesn't really risk her life (or, for that matter, her freedom or livelihood) by talking to him.

His system of quid pro quo exacts a psychological toll. While not painless, it is, according to our definitions, low cost. This will change at the climax when Clarice must confront a different serial killer, "in the open," without the security of prison bars to protect her.

This example raises a key point: action movies, thrillers, mysteries, dramas, and fantasy & science-fiction shouldn't end in cell #2 (or, for that matter, cell #1). To create a captivating finale, you must raise the cost of participation and shift into cell #3 (or possibly cell #4) by the time the climax begins in earnest.

To learn more about cells #3 and #4, keep reading!

- chapter six -

CELL #3:
HIGH COST,
SAFETY NEEDS

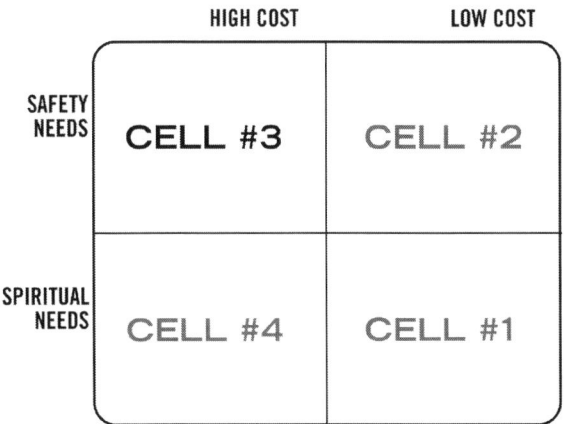

Cell #3 of the story stake matrix pairs safety need stakes with a high cost of participation.

169

From now onward, our discussion of the story stake matrix will exclude comedies, romances, and romantic comedies, and focus exclusively on action movies, etc.

Again, this is because, by definition, comedies and romantic comedies can't allow their protagonists to engage in high-cost activities. Not when these stories are supposed to be amusing and lighthearted.

To be in cell #3 (or #4), the danger to the hero has to feel real. Your comedy or romance will only fall into these two cells if you're writing a hybrid like an action comedy, romantic thriller, romantic drama, or comedic drama.

If that's the case, to craft an emotionally compelling story, combine, as needed, the success strategies from the appropriate story stake matrix cell.

If you're writing a romance novel that is *not* a hybrid in the vein of *The Bodyguard* or *Titanic*, your story may shift into cells #3 or #4. But those kinds of stories will not be discussed here. For guidance on how to handle them, please refer back to the special note for romance novelists (found within chapter 5).

Now that we've got that out of the way, let's explore cell #3!

Beginning Act 2A in Cell #3

Launching your second act from cell #3 is tricky. It certainly makes for a gripping start, that's for sure.

But if you begin with safety needs at stake *and* with a high cost of participation, it's difficult to raise the stakes later on. Not impossible, mind you, just difficult.

You probably only have to worry about this if you're writing a story with an "on the run" plot. Act 2A will typically begin with an exciting and dangerous chase sequence, with the hero being pursued by a member of law enforcement, the villain, or one of the villain's henchmen.

Of course, the chase can't last forever. Eventually, you'll have to slow down the pace, and take your hero to a place of relative safety. This gives him (and audiences) a chance to recuperate from all the action. (Alternatively, you can also shine the story spotlight on other characters who are engaged in less vigorous activities.) Either way, your story will slide back into cell #2, for a little while at least.

If your hero gets caught, he'll either be killed or sent to prison, maybe be put under mind control. Clearly, these consequences are extremely negative. So how do you raise the stakes at the midpoint?

You don't.

Not technically. Technically, you put a new slant on the cost of participation. That is, you change your hero's strategy from *defensive* to *offensive*.

To increase the tension within your story, your hero should voluntarily abandon his safe spot and venture out into the open, ideally to a location where he's most likely to be recognized and apprehended.

Because he can get caught at any second, because anything can be a potential threat, *everything* he does is a high-cost activity.

Whether he's snooping through someone's mail or buying a drink from a convenience store, danger is constantly lurking in the background. It's the hover effect on steroids!

This way, even when your hero isn't dodging bullets, audiences are going to be worried for his safety. This means that you can still fulfill genre requirements, while minimizing the potential for audiences to suffer from "action fatigue."

Although suspense tends to fatigue audiences less rapidly than action stunts, nevertheless, audiences can't remain under this degree of tension for too long. It will put a strain on their nerves and detract from their overall experience.

Again, for pacing reasons, every so often, even when your hero's out in the open, shift your story back into cell #2. Bring him to a place where he can temporarily be at ease, giving him (and audiences) a chance to relax. You might consider doing this immediately prior to the climax, when your story will shift into high gear yet again.

As you may've concluded, on-the-run plots spend more time in cell #3 than any other kind of story. This is why, when done well, they contain so much commercial appeal. Keeping audiences at the edge of their seats, these stories elicit a strong emotional response for sustained periods of time. The intensity of audience experience thus paves the way for rave reviews and word-of-mouth recommendations.

9 Ways to Make Your High-Stake Climax Even More of a Nail-Biter

Your hero is about to embark on a high-stake showdown, which will endanger his life, freedom, or livelihood.

With things already so tense, how can you make audiences care about the outcome of the climax a little more? How can you pull their emotional strings tauter?

First, perhaps, we should address why you should even bother with this extra step. Audiences, remember, are judging your story by its ability to make them feel. If you can wring out even an extra drop of emotion from them at this critical time, your story is going to be more powerful and compelling than the stories that don't implement these tactics.

As I said earlier, for a screenplay, this could mean the difference between a pass and a sale; for a novel, it could mean the difference between a three- or four-star review and a five.

So, if you want to elevate yourself above the competition, consider implementing one of the tactics below prior to (or, if appropriate, during) your story climax:

(1) Add in stakes of demise to the general stakes already in play.

Give the hero a deeply personal reason to participate in the climax. He's not just risking his life to save the hostages, city, or planet, but also to save someone precious to him.

If you're strongly resistant to this idea because, so often, the hero's loved one gets captured right before the climax, remember Len Wiseman's *Live Free or Die Hard* commentary. Audiences have a much easier time connecting to a personal mission than to a general one. A stronger connection will yield a better review—and all the benefits attendant on that.

Rather counterintuitively, the reverse—beginning with stakes of demise and then adding in stakes of general protection later on—tends to feel anticlimactic. It's the equivalent of telling someone, "Your wife is missing. Oh, and by the way, the fate of the world is at stake too!"

If you want to focus on your hero first, and bring in general stakes afterward, then at least foreshadow their advent.

In *Avatar*, for example, when audiences see the brightly colored arrows sticking out from machinery owned by the military base, they know that there is a larger conflict going on. Right away, they realize that this story is going to encompass something more than Jake's personal goal to gain freedom from being paraplegic.

Also, keep in mind that if your story, like *Taken* or *The Fugitive*, starts out highly personal, it's difficult to make it more personal, without veering into melodramatic territory. Instead, to keep audience involvement at peak levels, try one of the other approaches discussed below.

(2) Incorporate stakes of reputation.

One effective (but often overlooked) way to escalate tension during the climax is to explore stakes of reputation, specifically the concept of legacy.

In some cases, the hero will actively jeopardize his legacy in order to save others. As aforementioned, in *A Few Good Men*, Kaffee must elicit a confession from Colonel Jessep during the courtroom climax. If he doesn't, Kaffee will likely be court-martialed. The disgrace of it all will tarnish the family name and the vaunted legacy of his father, a famous lawyer and former US attorney general.

Audiences would be rooting for Kaffee to succeed anyway. He is likeable; Jessep is smug; and the defendants are innocent. But audiences root *even harder* for Kaffee's success because they know he is putting his father's legacy (as well as his own career) at risk in order to prevent two men from being unjustly convicted of murder. Since the personal costs to Kaffee are so high, audiences are more engaged by the climax than they would've been if only the fate of the defendants had been involved.

In other cases, legacy is not a cost, but a stake. The hero's participation in the climax doesn't endanger his legacy, but rather, should preserve it. We already saw one example of this with *Iron Man*. An even better one can be found in *Batman Begins*.

When Bruce Wayne's father was murdered, he left behind a legacy consisting of four components: his grieving son, the family name, Wayne Manor, and Gotham City itself. In regard to the fourth item, he used his wealth and influence to transform the decaying city into a place that thrived and flourished once more.

Before the climax begins, the villain causes Bruce to engage in behavior that brings disrepute to the Wayne family name; burns down the manor in a fire; and almost kills Bruce himself. Being a villain, naturally, he is not satisfied with all of this devastation. Three out of four isn't enough; he intends to destroy Gotham City too.

Thus, at the climax, Bruce (as Batman) must save Gotham City. This is a worthwhile stake in and of itself, and quite captivating on its lonesome. The fact that this city is part of his father's legacy, however, adds an extra layer of depth and nuance to Bruce's actions. This dynamic makes the climax much more emotionally rich than if only stakes of general protection had been in play.

Using stakes of reputation is one of the easiest ways to distinguish your climax from countless others. All you have to do is reflect on the nature of your hero's legacy, periodically refer to it throughout your story, and then, prior to the climax, draw audience attention to it in some way.

Pretty painless, and well worth your effort!

(3) Explore stakes of regret.

Your story climax will be more poignant if the actions your hero must engage in will redeem him from past failure. In other words, the climax isn't just about saving someone, it's also your hero's chance to atone and make amends.

Like stakes of reputation, adding stakes of regret to your story is fairly simple and straightforward. Again, you must first reflect on your hero's backstory and how you're going to communicate the relevant details to audiences.

Second, you must construct the actual climax so that it echoes his past failure literally (as in *In the Line of Fire*) or symbolically (as in *The Silence of the Lambs*).

Additionally, you can also explore the missed opportunity variation of regret. As discussed earlier, the universality of this feeling adds extra resonance to a situation that's already highly charged.

Give the stakes a keener emotional edge; create your own version of asking Rosie Cotton to dance.

(4) Remind audiences about the stakes.

This tactic may seem like it's too simple and obvious to be effective, but it really does work. Not only that, if reminders are lacking from the climax, audiences definitely feel their absence.

Remember though, that it's most efficacious when you remind audiences about the stakes through images rather than through dialogue.

(5) Generate stakes of justice.

Prior to the climax (and in some cases, during it), have the villain or one of his henchmen kill someone who is precious to the hero. (Or, alternatively, devise another heinous crime for the villain to commit.)

This should recharge audience interest in seeing the villain defeated, making audiences even more invested in the outcome of the climax than they already were.

Note: If stakes of justice are not combined with a safety need stake, then your climax actually falls into cell #4 (which we will get to, in due course).

(6) Foreshadow future stakes.

To do this, hint that if the hero fails to overcome the villain in the present, someone else's life will be at stake in the future.

This works even if the threat isn't explicitly conveyed to the hero. As long as audiences are aware of this potential danger, another undercurrent of tension will heighten whatever they're already feeling.

In *Gladiator* and *Minority Report*, the villains not only have jeopardized the freedom of their worlds (stakes of general protection) but also have victimized the hero quite horrifically (stakes of justice). For these reasons, audiences would already be substantially invested in the outcome of the climax.

These films deepen that investment even further by giving audiences yet another thing to worry about. If Maximus fails to defeat Commodus in *Gladiator*, Rome will never become a republic; Maximus will fail to avenge the murder of his wife and son; *and*, quite possibly, Commodus will kill his own young nephew.

In *Minority Report*, if Anderton doesn't expose Burgess, the Precrime program will spread its pernicious tentacles across the nation; Anderton will be framed for a murder he did not intend to commit (a murder Burgess hoped to engineer by preying on Anderton's grief over his dead son); *and*, quite possibly, in order to protect himself, Burgess might kill Anderton's wife.

(7) Prior to the climax, boost the likeability of either the hero or the stakes.

To get audiences to root even harder for the hero to rescue the stakes, enhance the likeability of either party.

This is often accomplished by having the hero (or the stakes) demonstrating kindness or sympathy toward others. Since the hero (or the stakes) are in a precarious situation themselves, these acts of generosity are especially emotionally resonant.

In *The Fugitive*, Dr. Kimble has been falsely convicted of murdering his wife. He is likeable, sympathetic, and innocent. From the very beginning, audiences are rooting for him to find the real murderer and clear his own name. It seems almost impossible for them to be more invested in his plight.

Almost impossible.

Disguised as a janitor, Kimble sneaks into a hospital to find information that could lead him to the murderer. While there, he realizes that a young boy has been misdiagnosed. Kimble takes the time to alter the child's medical chart and to transport the boy to the correct operating room.

Logically, Kimble should be worried about his own safety. The longer he lingers in the hospital, the more likely it is that he'll be detected. Because he places his own life at risk to save the boy's, Kimble's likeability—already high—approaches stratospheric levels. As a result, audiences root even harder for his success.

Although effective, likeability boosters do come with a major drawback. Like some of the reminder strategies we discussed earlier on, they can affect your story's momentum. If you want to use this tactic, be careful.

Don't make your hero go completely outside of the trajectory of your story to help another person. In *The Fugitive*, Kimble has good reason to venture into the hospital in the first place. His likeability booster evolves from that initial motivation, which was already strong.

(8) Make use of stakes of sacrifice.

Prior to the climax, have your hero make a significant sacrifice.

That way, going into the climax, audiences know that if the hero fails, this sacrifice will have been made in vain.

This adds an extra layer of poignancy to the climax itself, which again, bolsters its ability to elicit emotion from audiences.

(9) Draw audience attention to boundaries of time, resources, or magic.

The climax is the time to go beyond a deadline, tighten the hero's restrictions, and incorporate a ticking clock. (Remember, it doesn't have to be a literal clock.)

Make sure to cut away to it every now and again. If you don't remind audiences about it, you're not going to achieve the desired effect.

If you haven't included a clock, reconsider.

It creates urgency that amplifies the tension audiences are already feeling due to the stakes currently in play. Without a clock, you're leaving a significant advantage on the table. It's like going to a free buffet, and sampling everything except for the ultra-expensive jumbo prawn cocktail.

Additionally, you can draw attention to the depletion of the hero's resources as well as to his vulnerabilities to certain types of magic. While these also intensify audience emotion, most of the time, they're still not going to be as powerful as a ticking clock.

Avoiding the Anticlimactic Ending

High stakes plus high-cost action. Sounds like a recipe for a captivating climax, doesn't it?

And it is.

But *both* components need to be present in order to avoid an anticlimactic ending. (There are a few other elements to consider too, but these, I'm afraid, are beyond the scope of the story stake matrix.)

Your story, in short, needs to remain squarely in cell #3 (or possibly #4) for the vast majority of its grand finale.

If safety needs are at stake, *you need to keep them in play until the very end of your climax.*

Writers, for some reason, have the propensity to take the stakes out of play prematurely. Perhaps, they have come to identify with the stakes so strongly that they can't bear to keep the stakes in extreme danger for too long.

Whatever the cause, the result is the same: when you take the stakes out of harm's way, your climax is over. Whether you intended to or not, you're transitioning into the resolution of your story.

Bear in mind, you just need to keep *something* at stake. It doesn't necessarily have to be the same thing. If you take one set of safety need stakes out of play, but put a new set into play, you're still golden.

In *Robin Hood: Prince of Thieves*, once Robin saves a band of Sherwood folk (including Little John's son) from the hangman's noose, these stakes go out of play.

But the climax is not over, because the Sheriff of Nottingham's darkly ambitious plans continue to threaten Lady Marian (stakes of demise) as well as the future of England (stakes of general protection). Both of these stakes help fuel the rest of the climax, although, it should be noted, that the latter doesn't carry nearly as much emotional weight as the former.

In *Face/Off*, during one part of the film's lengthy climax, the life of the hero's wife is at stake. When she is brought to relative safety, new stakes are put into play. The hero's daughter suddenly materializes—surprise!—and now, her life too, is at stake.

The daughter manages to injure the villain, and he runs off. The immediacy of the danger is gone, but, nevertheless, the villain still poses a threat to the hero's family. This future possibility sustains the rest of the climax—along with the hero's need for payback (which broaches cell #4 territory).

Before we delve into the intricacies of cell #4, we've got to address the second key component of a riveting climax: the cost of participation.

You might begin the climactic sequence with a low-cost activity such as preparation, but your hero's actions need to escalate into riskier endeavors that have the potential to injure life, limb, and future.

Due to the danger they entail, these high-cost activities should also help you fulfill genre requirements, providing audiences with the action, drama, or thrills they paid to experience. Without the genre goods, audiences are going to be disappointed. To them, the climax will feel anticlimactic—no matter how long the stakes remain in play.

Consider the thriller *Fracture*. Smart and stylish in several respects, it's full of engaging, "cat and mouse" encounters between the protagonist (district attorney Willy Beachum) and the villain (wealthy engineer Ted Crawford). Unfortunately, the final confrontation between the two men—which, as part of the climax, should be the most thrilling—is one of the least compelling encounters of the bunch.

To see why, let's analyze the film with the story stake matrix. At the beginning, Crawford shoots his adulteress wife, who's in a coma for most of the movie. Thus, her tragic condition fires up stakes of justice.

During Act 2A, to achieve this justice, Beachum engages in low-cost activities, mainly: (a) arguing with a police detective about the missing murder weapon, and (b) visiting Crawford in jail to discuss issues with Crawford's confession. With this combination of spiritual need stakes and low costs, the story remains in cell #1.

But after the midpoint, the costs rise. If Beachum fails to convict Crawford, Beachum can say good-bye to his new (and lucrative) job with a corporate law firm. Due to the enormity of such a failure, he wouldn't be able to return to his old job with the district attorney's office, either. Did I mention Beachum has thousands of dollars in student loan debt to pay?

These are high costs. Combined with stakes of justice, after the midpoint, the story falls into cell #4. Critically, however, it doesn't stay there. At the end of the climax, when Beachum confronts Crawford at Crawford's home, these costs have disappeared.

At this point, due to lack of evidence, Crawford has been acquitted. Beachum has lost the case, his corporate law position, and his job with the D.A.'s office. Technically, the lattermost is re-offered to him, but he declines to accept it.

But, in the grand scheme of things, this technicality isn't of consequence. No matter how you look at it, when Beachum enters Crawford's home, Beachum's career is not on the line.

Let's examine another high-cost option: risking freedom. Does Beachum risk imprisonment by confronting Crawford?

The answer to this question depends on whether audiences believe Beachum might kill Crawford to obtain justice on behalf of Crawford's wife. If so, Beachum could potentially be convicted of murder himself, and consequently, be sent to prison.

At this stage of the story, Crawford's wife is no longer in a coma; she's dead. Crawford pulled the plug on her life support, and Beachum failed to stop him. Even worse, Crawford exhibits no remorse over the way he killed her, even going so far as to taunt Beachum about the vacation he's taking, a second honeymoon, which "won't be the same" without his wife.

The egregiousness of Crawford's crime, coupled with the callousness of his attitude, gives credence to the idea that Beachum might be driven to kill Crawford. This idea is further reinforced in two key ways.

Moments before the final climactic confrontation, Beachum says to his former boss, "I let a man get away with murder. How am I supposed to live with that?" Then, during the confrontation itself, the film occasionally zooms in on a gun Beachum has found on Crawford's premises and keeps at his side, as if to imply Beachum could deploy it at any second.

Yet, despite these hints, it's difficult to believe that Beachum will shoot Crawford. While Beachum appears to be haunted by this case (unlike the man Crawford's wife was having the affair with, who, incidentally, committed suicide earlier on), Beachum doesn't have a deeply personal connection to the victim.

More important, through images of Beachum reading law textbooks and through gestures Beachum makes at police headquarters right before he visits Crawford's home, it's indicated that he's gleaned fresh insight into the case.

Although audiences don't know what it is exactly, they know Beachum has some new trick up his sleeve. He's not arriving on Crawford's doorstep completely "empty-handed."

In other words, he's not at the end of his rope. He's not desperate enough to kill Crawford and lose his own freedom for the sake of justice. Everything signals that Beachum has found an intellectual solution to this mess—not a suicidal one.

This high cost is out…leaving us with death. To stop Beachum from taking him down, Crawford could theoretically kill Beachum. After all, Crawford already shot his wife—and got away with it. What's to prevent him from doing the same to Beachum?

Crawford's own calculating personality, that's what.

Crawford's crime was not committed out of passion. He shot his wife cold-bloodedly, having meticulously planned its execution—and his escape—down to every last detail. It would be a major betrayal of his character (not to mention a major cheat) for him to kill Beachum in a fit of hot-headed rage now.

True, it can be argued that Crawford has lured Beachum to his house to pull a similar stunt. That is, kill Beachum in such a way that Crawford can, as he did with his wife's murder, get away with the crime.

But again, Crawford's personality rules out this possibility too. He is arrogant, smug, convinced of his own invulnerability. He's unlikely to go to such lengths when he's concluded that he's won the game, while Beachum, on the other hand, has lost, and hence, no longer poses a threat.

Time to look at our final tally. We've crossed off the loss of livelihood, freedom, and life as potential high costs. This means that Beachum engages in low-cost activities at the tail end of the climax, placing it squarely in cell #1.

We're in anticlimax territory—a death knell for any thriller.

To underscore this point, let's contrast *Fracture*'s ending with the final confrontation between Kaffee and Jessep in *A Few Good Men*. Interestingly, it's possible Beachum's own character was heavily inspired by Kaffee's. Unlike Kaffee, who plea bargains his cases away, Beachum takes his cases to court.

But their behavior is manifestation of the same flaw: both men are afraid to lose. Instead, they content themselves with numerous, but shallow, victories. By the end of their journeys, these two protagonists will overcome their fears and put their talents to good use.

Nonetheless, despite this intriguing parallel, *Men*'s final climactic encounter is more riveting—by a wide margin too.

Why?

At the end of *Men*, as we've previously discussed, Kaffee puts his own career on the line to save two marines. This high cost, paired with safety need stakes, places the final courtroom showdown in cell #3. (*Note*: Kaffee's also jeopardizing his father's legacy, but this doesn't put the showdown in cell #3. It does, however, enhance the resonance and intensity of the encounter.)

And so, when Kaffee is interrogating Jessep on the stand, audiences are at the edge of their seats. They're wondering if Kaffee (who seems to be floundering) will be able to acquit his defendants. But more than that, they're wondering if he has badly miscalculated, if he has taken a risky gamble with his career and is about to lose big. This climax is enthralling, through and through.

The same can't be said for *Fracture*. Superficially, with atmospheric lighting and music (and the close-ups of the gun by Beachum's side), the end of the climax has the hallmarks of a thriller…but it's all smoke and mirrors.

Yes, the stakes are both emotionally compelling and in play until the very end. Even so, Beachum's cost of participation—unlike

Kaffee's—is low. Consequently, audiences are unlikely to be in suspense over the outcome of Beachum's final encounter with Crawford.

In sum, while the film's ending is certainly poetic (if Crawford hadn't insisted on pulling the plug on his wife's life support, he'd still be untouchable), it's not very thrilling. Ultimately, it fails to satisfy.

The lack of high costs is the troublemaker here. If present, *Fracture*'s ending would be greatly improved because, in this story, the stakes of justice are powerful enough to warrant high-cost action.

This isn't always the case with spiritual need stakes, as we'll see in the next chapter…

- chapter seven -

CELL #4:
HIGH COST,
SPIRITUAL NEEDS

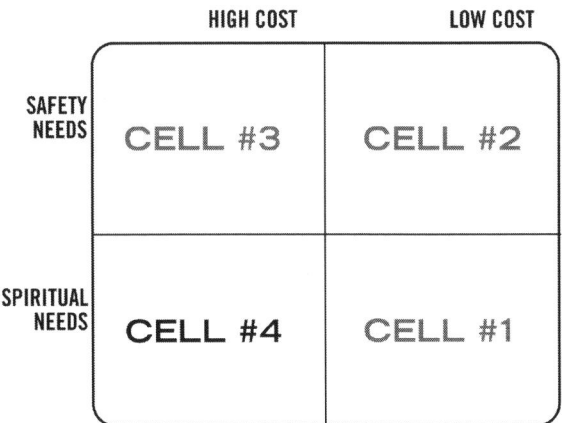

Cell #4 of the story stake matrix pairs spiritual need stakes with a high cost of participation.

IF ANY PART OF YOUR STORY—ESPECIALLY THE climax—is categorized by this cell, you must proceed with caution.

Unlike cell #2, the misalignment between the cost of participation and the needs it fulfills can bother audiences. And for good reason. You're veering into the territory of reckless endangerment.

Your hero is purposefully courting the loss of livelihood, freedom, even life—and for what?

For the sake of love. Perhaps justice or reputation, or for esteem.

While these stakes certainly enrich human existence, in the world of movies (and novels), they just don't elicit the same kind of emotional response and level of understanding as safety need stakes.

Accordingly, you've got to become the Ogilvy of creative writing.

You've got to "sell it."

Really, really sell it.

You've got to make audiences believe that the dangers the hero is about to face are worth the rewards.

Alternatively, you *must* add in new stakes, shifting from spiritual needs to safety needs, thereby moving your story into the safe zone of cell #3.

Pictorially, your options look something like the diagram on the next page:

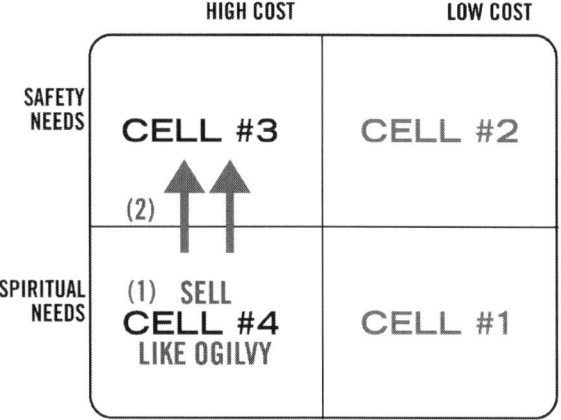

Cell #4 stories are tricky. You must (1) emulate famous advertising executive David Ogilvy and convince audiences that the stakes justify the high-cost risks. If this proves too difficult, consider (2) raising the stakes, i.e. shifting your story into cell #3, where no "selling" is required.

Selling it is not as easy as it may sound. Hopefully, the examples in this chapter will help clarify what you must do to get audiences to buy into your protagonist's high-cost actions.

Selling Stakes of Justice

To invoke stakes of justice, the villain must commit a heinous crime against the hero, and the hero's journey, consequently, is about exacting payback.

Alternatively, the villain may perpetrate an awful crime, not necessarily against the hero, but the hero is, nevertheless, willing to risk his job (or pay another high cost), in order to bring the villain to justice.

If the crime is heinous enough, and if audiences experience it firsthand, stakes of justice are usually enough to fuel the entire second act.

Keep in mind, though, that three other factors play a role:

- bonding with the victim
- time elapse
- the initial threshold of the costs

If the victim is presented as likeable or sympathetic, and if his value to the hero is clearly demonstrated, then audiences will be more likely to understand why the hero is so motivated to seek justice.

Even so, the effect of a heinous crime on audience emotion wanes over time. Furthermore, as the costs to the hero escalate, it may seem like he's foolish to risk his own life in order to avenge someone who is already dead (no matter how likeable or sympathetic the victim is).

For these reasons, generally speaking, it's at the climax where you hit a sticky wicket.

If the heinous crime is committed during Act One, the climax is going to be separated from it by a wide interval. Additionally, fulfilling genre requirements during this particular sequence requires the hero to face maximum danger. Such risky behavior may appear unwarranted, especially if, at this point, audiences have forgotten how likeable or sympathetic the victim is.

To put these concepts in perspective, let's take a look at *Beverly Hills Cop*. During the film's beginning, one of the villain's henchmen murders Michael, a friend of detective Axel Foley. Since Michael had been living in Beverly Hills, Foley decides to journey there to discover who is responsible for his friend's death.

Before Foley leaves, his boss issues him a stern warning. If his boss finds out that Foley has been conducting any kind of investigation during "the vacation" Foley requested, he will fire Foley. Right away, audiences know that Foley's pursuit of justice is a high-cost endeavor.

And they are totally onboard with the idea!

How does the film accomplish this feat?

Through a variety of techniques:

- Audiences see the murder firsthand. (It isn't shunted offscreen; it isn't described to them by witnesses after the fact.)
- Although Foley and Michael haven't seen each other in a long time, they were friends during childhood.
- Michael even covered for Foley when they were 15 years old and got caught stealing a car. (It was a Cadillac, BTW!)

Taken together, all of these details sell audiences on the idea that the risk to Foley (the loss of his livelihood) is worth the reward (stakes of justice). Because of this understanding, audiences not only support Foley's decision, they root even harder for him to succeed!

This choice is the mark of a professional. An amateur would've been content that he created a personal relationship between Foley and the victim. An amateur would be delighted with the premise of a wiseass Detroit cop venturing off into ritzy Beverly Hills to solve a case (which, admittedly, is a good premise).

An amateur would've been so pleased with himself that he would've stopped there. He would've had Foley begin his jaunt to Beverly Hills *with his boss's blessing*. This, you'll note, would mean that the second act would begin in cell #1.

A pro, on the other hand, will not be content with a good concept. He'll want to make minor alterations to it, to transform it into something great.

In this case, the pros introduced a high cost early on, shifting the second act into cell #4. This choice makes the negative consequences of failure even worse—from the very beginning of Act 2A—which, in turn, raises the stakes and deepens audience engagement. The simple inclusion of a high cost, in other words, generated a more powerful second act.

Before the climax, the costs will rise again. Bogomil, a lieutenant with the Beverly Hills police force, orders one of his officers to escort Foley to the city limits. Bogomil warns Foley that if he returns to Beverly Hills, Foley will be prosecuted to the fullest extent of the law.

By continuing his investigation, Foley not only risks unemployment, but also incarceration. Because audiences admire Foley for his willingness to risk so much, again, they become more invested in his goal.

During the climax, however, this admiration could've easily soured. The whole house of cards could've potentially collapsed.

Look at what Foley has to do: he must storm the villain's mansion.

A mansion protected by a bevy of security guards.

Security guards with machine guns.

Except for two Beverly Hills cops, who have little experience with serious crime, Foley has no backup.

The costs have become so high that stakes of justice can no longer warrant them.

If Foley blithely blazes into the villain's stronghold just to avenge Michael, Foley may appear brave, but he also comes across as foolish.

That is the kiss of death.

You never want audiences to have niggling thoughts, which question the hero's rationale for participating in the climax. Not even the ghost of a niggling thought. Not even the whisper of a ghost of a niggling thought.

If this happens, those doubts will color their entire experience of the climax. No matter how exciting the climax is, audiences will disengage from it. They won't be as emotionally involved as they would've been, had they not had cause to question your protagonist's participation at all.

Consequently, they'll be less inclined to wax enthusiastic about your story as a whole. Instead of rave reviews, you wind up with a lackluster response.

Of course, everything changes if there is a reason why Foley *cannot* walk away from the climax. And the movie supplies one: Jenny.

A childhood friend of both Foley and Michael, she's been taken hostage by the villain. If Foley doesn't storm the mansion now, Jenny will die. Foley absolutely cannot wait for backup.

In sum, stakes of demise were added to the stakes of justice already in play. Now, with this addition, the stakes justify the risks. Audiences can fully and wholeheartedly invest in Foley's (and the two other officers') attempts to infiltrate the mansion and rescue Jenny.

To put it another way, in order to create a riveting ending, the story had to shift into cell #3 immediately prior to the climax. It couldn't remain in cell #4.

Could the climax be sustained by stakes of justice alone? It's hard to say.

Perhaps, if audiences had, firsthand, seen Michael cover for Foley when the two had been caught stealing the Cadillac, if audiences knew that this generosity had ruined Michael's own dreams of becoming a cop, and if Foley is plagued with guilt over what had happened, then maybe the climax could've worked without bringing Jenny into the equation.

That's a lot of ifs.

Even with them, it's still a close call. If you ever doubt whether stakes of justice, by themselves, could sustain your climax, do yourself a favor.

Move your story out of cell #4 and into cell #3. Add in safety need stakes, so that the rewards match the level of risks, and audiences have no reason to question your hero's judgment.

Actually, this will give you the best of both worlds. With the inclusion of stakes of demise (or another safety need stake), an extra layer of tension will be added to the climax. Audiences will be even *more* emotionally involved in its outcome than if only stakes of justice were in play.

As an alternative option, use the power of time elapse to your advantage. Have the villain kill someone precious to the hero immediately prior to the climax. This way, the interval between the heinous crime and the climax itself will be brief. So brief, in fact, that the effect of the former should be strong enough to fuel the latter.

Selling Stakes of Reputation

If stakes of reputation are tied to safety need stakes, as a general rule, you don't have to do any selling. Audiences will be worried that someone might die or go to jail or be unable to make a living. The fact that a reputation also hangs in the balance adds extra depth to the tension already present.

Things get a bit tricky, however, when stakes of reputation function as a spiritual need stake—and the hero has to engage in high-cost activities to preserve it.

To illustrate, let's examine *National Treasure 2: Book of Secrets*. Ben Gates is on yet another treasure hunt, this time for Cibola, a lost city of gold. But—and again, this is the mark of a pro—he's not in it only for the money.

At the film's outset, Ben's ancestor is implicated in the assassination of Abraham Lincoln. In a convoluted bit of logic, the discovery of the city would clear this ancestor's name, preventing it from being turned "to mud."

When the costs are moderate, these stakes of reputation can sustain the action. It's easy to buy into the idea that Ben would fly to Paris to clear the name of his ancestor. It might be less easy to buy into the idea that Ben would sneak into Buckingham Palace *and* the Oval Office to locate clues to the treasure, but it's feasible.

In short, the concept of legacy is enough to pull the story forward during Act 2A. But things start to crumble once the movie hits Act 2B, when the costs start to escalate.

See, the president knows the location of a special (and somewhat mythical) book that contains a facsimile of the last clue Ben needs to find the treasure.

To get the book, and hence the clue, Ben decides to kidnap the president.

Yes, the president of the United States.

That's when the stakes, in combination with the costs, crash into a brick wall.

As everyone knows, bad things happen to people who try to go after the president. Ben is actively risking imprisonment—or worse—and why?

To get his hands on a clue, which should lead him to a treasure, which, in turn, will clear his ancestor's name. Ben's ancestor is long dead. His reputation does not significantly impact Ben's present (or future) or the present (or future) of the people Ben loves. The costs outweigh the stakes, and it's virtually impossible to sell audiences on the idea.

Now, this misstep didn't hurt the film's box office success any. There are several reasons for this:

- Goodwill from the first film carried over into the sequel.
- Children in the audience (and some adults) would be enthralled by the sheer verve of Ben's plan.
- The Secret Service agents don't appear that menacing, which helps downplay the risk Ben is taking.
- Actors Nic Cage and Bruce Greenwood delivered compelling performances.

That last one is the most important. Nic and Bruce sell audiences on the sequence.

But, I would not recommend this approach if you're trying to sell a spec screenplay or publish your novel. The actors won't be there to do the selling for you.

You've got to rely on your writing alone.

In the case of *National Treasure 2*, the easiest way to do this is to move the story out of cell #4. That is, add in safety need stakes and shift the story into cell #3.

For instance, the villain could get ahold of Ben's mother and threaten to harm her if Ben doesn't provide him with the last clue. Now, Ben has to kidnap the president, not just for the treasure (stakes of happiness), not just to restore the good name of his long-dead ancestor (stakes of reputation), but also to save his own mother (stakes of demise).

With our addition, the costs are in alignment with the stakes, and audiences can happily enjoy Ben's kidnapping caper without reservation.

As a matter of fact, in the film, a variation of this actually happens immediately prior to the climax—but critically—*after* the kidnapping. We've just changed the timing of the villain's threat to create a more effective story.

Do you see the difference?

Instead of having the plot go there (the kidnapping stunt) because the filmmakers *wanted* it to go there, we made it so that the story couldn't go anywhere *but* there.

No one can complain that our hero is testing all bounds of credibility and, as a result, put down our story in disgust.

To be fair to *National Treasure 2*, after the stunt with the president, the risks and stakes did match. The president can't tell anyone why Ben kidnapped him because the book of secrets is supposed to stay…well…secret.

In another bit of convoluted (but buyable) logic, Ben must find the treasure to avoid going to jail for trying to kidnap the leader of the free world. The threat of imprisonment has transformed into a stake. To put it another way, Ben's no longer actively courting incarceration. Instead, he's trying to *avoid* a lengthy sentence in Leavenworth.

A subtle difference, but an important one.

It means that Ben has yet another motivation to find the lost city of Cibola. When his final pursuit of it threatens his life (as well as the lives of the people he loves), audiences won't think he jolly well deserves it. They could've potentially felt that way, if he were only motivated by greed, or by foolish (if noble) sentiments about his ancestor's legacy.

Instead, because Ben is propelled into the final search for the treasure by the desire to save his mom (stakes of demise) *and* avoid jail (stakes of freedom), audiences are still onboard with him.

Because the stakes have been raised, audiences do not deem him a fool and disengage from his quest. Quite the opposite. They are more invested in his plight than ever before. Hence, they will remain under tension, at the edge of their seats, until they know that he's reached safe ground.

Selling Stakes of Happiness

In the case of *National Treasure 2*, we added in stakes of demise to make it plausible that the hero would risk incarceration for the sake of his goal. This shifted the story into cell #3, and raises a good question.

Can heroes be willing to risk incarceration merely for spiritual need stakes?

Sure. But you have to be able to—you guessed it—sell it.

We've actually discussed an example of this earlier on: *Ocean's Eleven*. Here, let's delve into more specifics.

At first, audiences think the casino heist is mostly about the money and partly about getting back at the house, "who always wins." The latter is a nice sentiment. Coupled with the likeability and charisma of Danny Ocean's con men crew, it's enough to sustain the first half of the film's second act.

Then, the guys are participating in low-cost activities, like conducting reconnaissance missions and building a decoy vault. But in Act 2B, the costs start to rise. The guys have to steal an expensive device from a local university—not to mention pull off the heist itself.

You could argue that the size of the pot—$160 million—is worth the risks. But remember, stories in which the hero endangers his life or freedom just for money tend not to be emotionally compelling. As for the vague idea that the guys are getting back at the house? That no longer cuts it either.

Audiences need something more to keep them invested in the heist. At the midpoint, when their interest could dwindle, the movie gives them another reason to care: Danny's ex-wife, Tess.

That's when audiences learn that Terry Benedict, owner of the three casinos the crew is targeting, is none other than Tess's new boyfriend. Now, Danny isn't actively courting another prison sentence just to pull off a million dollar heist; he's also doing it to win back the heart of his ex-wife.

Like money, pursuit of love generates stakes of hero happiness. Thus, even with this addition, we still have a combination of high costs and spiritual need stakes. The film is still in cell #4.

The big difference, though, is that it's a lot easier to get audiences to root for love than it is to get them to root for money.

So, how exactly do the filmmakers sell audiences on the idea of love? Here are a few of their tricks:

- Danny continues to wear his wedding ring.
- At the demolition of Reuben's old casino, when everyone's watching the destruction, Danny's gaze is squarely on Tess.
- Linus says the best part of his day is watching Tess. (This supplements the idea that she's a catch, and therefore, worth the risks.)
- Tess and Danny's conversations sizzle with chemistry.
- Benedict is not the kind of man Tess believes him to be (and their relationship is showing cracks at the seams).

In combination, all of these details convince audiences that the risk (imprisonment) is worth the rewards (the millions *and* Tess). Audiences are totally onboard with the scheme, rooting even harder for the charismatic crew to succeed.

And so, at the end, when Danny (who was sent back to prison for violating parole) is released and walks out into the fresh air, with his millions and his ex-wife waiting for him, audiences won't watch the credits scroll down the screen, while thinking he was a fool for trying.

Instead, like Danny himself, they'll say to themselves, "Man, that was worth it. It was really, really worth it!"

- chapter eight -

THE STORY STAKE MATRIX: WRAPPING UP

IN THIS CHAPTER, WE WILL ADDRESS SOME LOOSE ends pertaining to the story stake matrix and your implementation of it.

Specifically, we'll look at:

- final pointers that concern all cells in the matrix
- a basic version of the matrix that involves only four steps (!)
- resources to help you apply what you've learned

Ready to dive in?

Final Pointers for Cells #1–#4

After you've evaluated your plot through the lens of the story stake matrix, there are some last minute assessments to make.

You should double-check that:

(1) Your protagonist hasn't engaged in excessively callous behavior.

Although less than ideal, this usually isn't a deal-breaker in a plot driven by safety need stakes. But one excessively coldhearted act can kill a story that is solely fueled by stakes of hero happiness.

If your protagonist fails to achieve his goal, it's not the end of the world. He'll just be unhappy. That's all.

Emotional identification with him is holding your entire story together. Lose that, and your screenplay or novel will fall apart at the seams.

(2) Audience goodwill hasn't dissipated by the time your protagonist goes after his goal.

If you want to avoid fidgety audiences, make sure your protagonist takes concrete steps to achieve his goal by the 25% mark of your story (or thereabouts).

Audiences can't root for him to get the girl or save the world until he actually starts to play the game!

(3) Your protagonist has endured enough ordeals.

If life's been too easy for your protagonist during Act Two, as much as they like Nice (or Naughty) Ned, audiences will feel like he hasn't earned his Act Three reward.

Make him work for it.

Make sure he experiences a variety of obstacles that require either low or high costs to overcome.

The Basic Story Stake Action Plan

At this point, you might be thinking that the story stake matrix is…a little complicated.

I agree. It can be.

But as I said earlier, mastering it should yield rich dividends. Once you understand it, it will help you write the kind of story that keeps readers up at night, the kind of story that gets readers to rave about your work.

That being said, you may find a simpler approach more useful.

Voila!

Your wish is about to come true.

The principles behind the story stake matrix can be distilled into four core elements. I couldn't share this basic story stake action plan with you earlier, because in all honesty, it makes better sense when you've had a thorough introduction to the matrix, as a whole, first.

Now, you're prepped and ready.

So here it is:

(1) During Act One, spend time establishing the central story stakes.

(2) Periodically, raise the stakes by (a) increasing the cost of participation, and/or (b) putting new stakes into play. The best times to do this are usually at the midpoint and immediately prior to the climax.

(3) Whenever possible, weave modulating factors into the fabric of your story.

(4) Verify that the cost of participation is in alignment with the stakes. This is essential throughout Acts Two and Three, but it's especially so during the latter, when your hero will typically face the greatest level of danger.

That's it. That's the story stake matrix in a nutshell.

Sounds simple enough, doesn't it?

In fact, at first, you might feel more comfortable just using the basic story stake action plan to craft your plot (or, if you're a pantser, to evaluate your rough draft). If you adopt this approach, your screenplay or novel should be off to a solid start.

But to stand out in a crowded marketplace and give your readers the most intense emotional experience possible, you should treat the basic action plan as a supplement to the full story stake matrix (as discussed in chapters 4–7), rather than as a replacement for it.

Helpful Resources for You

There's no better time than the present to apply the knowledge you've learned so far!

Before reading the next chapter in this book, take a moment to download and fill out a free story stake worksheet made especially for you.

If writing exercises are more your style than worksheets, I've still got you covered. Take a few minutes to scribble down an answer to one of the writing exercises included in this section.

Both of these activities are, of course, completely optional. If you prefer, you can ignore them altogether, or perhaps, return to them after you've finished reading this writing guide. (By the way, you can easily return to this page from the table of contents.)

Free Story Stake Worksheet

If you're about to start, are in the middle of, or have just finished a rough draft of your screenplay or novel (or an outline for either), please take a look at the (printable) story stake worksheet that's available at my website.

Created just for readers of this writing guide, it will walk you, step by step, through a series of questions and checklists designed to help you perfectly develop the stakes in your story.

You can download it for free from here:

http://scribemeetsworld.com/stakes-worksheet/

3 Story Stake Exercises

If you aren't in the middle of a writing project, but would still like to apply the knowledge you've learned from this book, try one (or more) of the following exercises.

I hope this practice session will be one step on your path toward story stake domination!

Exercise #1: X-Men

At the climax of the film, several world dignitaries are about to be turned into blobs of jelly through a contraption devised by the villain.

Tensions rise as destructive rays emitted by the contraption come closer and closer to the assembled dignitaries. The fate of one of the heroes also hangs in the balance.

The stakes seem pretty high already, don't they?

And they are…but can you think of a way to wring even one more drop of emotion from audiences?

Hint: audiences haven't gotten to know the dignitaries. Try to incorporate one of them into the fabric of the plot so audiences form a bond with the general stakes, and correspondingly, will care even more about their fate.

Exercise #2: Four Christmases

Kate and Brad planned to spend Christmas relaxing in Fiji. But when their flight gets canceled, they're forced to spend the holiday with each of their parents.

Cry me a river.

Attractive and affluent, Kate and Brad are living the good life. Why should audiences care about their first-world problems?

Rewrite the beginning so that the hero and heroine come across as more likeable, sympathetic, or fascinating.

Exercise #3: Fool's Gold

This film has a decent premise: a divorced couple joins forces to find a lost treasure off the coast of the Bahamas. The problem (one of them at least) is with the stakes.

Give Tess and Finn another reason to go on a treasure hunt besides the fact that it's exciting, romantic, and lucrative.

Both have some debts to pay off, but as I recall, that angle isn't played up enough to truly count as a strong stake. Start from there, or create new stakes altogether.

If you're feeling really ambitious, give the Honeycutt family another reason to fund the hunt besides the fact that it's—say it with me—exciting, romantic, and lucrative.

• • •

If you've come this far, you'll be a pro at using story stakes to increase tension and sustain audience involvement in your screenplay or novel. Although these are "the biggies," there are other purposes for stakes. In the next chapter of this writing guide, we'll examine five additional uses for them.

- chapter nine -

5 ADDITIONAL PURPOSES FOR STORY STAKES

So far, we've focused on the central story stakes, the ones attached to your protagonist's overall goal, which provide the underlying motivation for the majority of his actions.

These stakes will dominate your story, keeping readers turning the pages and sustaining their emotional involvement with your plot and characters.

However, it's time for us to widen our gazes and examine how stakes can be used for other purposes.

In this chapter, we will specifically look at how stakes can be used to:

- craft a dynamic opening
- humanize the antagonist of your story
- provide relief from action or monotony

- create suspects and red herrings (in a mystery)
- advance your plot without sacrificing your characters

With that bird's eye view taken care of, let's dig a little deeper!

Craft a Dynamic Opening

Stakes create tension. Readers keep on reading to relieve this tension.

Hence, it stands to reason that opening your story with something at stake is a great way to secure reader interest from page 1.

Keep in mind that these initial story stakes usually don't drive the overall plot of your story (although they may be connected to it). They will quickly go out of play. This is just a short-term strategy. To grip audiences for the long haul, to keep them wholly invested, you must present the central story stakes sometime thereafter.

Also, unlike central story stakes, initial story stakes can still be effective even when audiences don't exactly know what the negative consequences of failure entail. As long as audiences get the vague sense that something bad will happen, your opening should possess enough tension to suck them into your story world.

Finally, the best openings accomplish multiple objectives. (This is especially crucial in screenplays, where you're limited to 120 pages.) The first sequence shouldn't just contain tension generated by the stakes. Ideally, it will also introduce the hero (or villain); fulfill genre requirements; and set up key details, which will become pertinent later on.

Take *Twister*, for example. It opens with a tense, brief prologue that shows the fate of a family at stake. They are desperately trying to reach their underground shelter as a tornado approaches.

The family consists of a young girl (the heroine as a child), her mom, her dad—and in a fantastic use of a modulating factor—their pet dog. Concern for the dog's safety makes this beginning at least 10 times tenser than it would've been without the inclusion of the little pet.

Besides generating enough tension to hook audiences from the get-go, notice that this opening *immediately* provides audiences with a glimpse of the special effects they came to see. Additionally, it introduces the heroine, while simultaneously overcoming a credibility hurdle, which could've arisen in the future.

Without it, audiences could question why the heroine, Jo, is willing to risk her life to chase tornadoes. To them, she might appear like an adrenaline junkie, who recklessly endangers her life for kicks. Sure, she's trying to gather data that will enable a more accurate forecasting system. But because her later predicaments are so extreme, her motives could've been suspect.

Since Jo's dad died in the disaster showcased in the prologue, everyone understands why she's willing to risk so much to get this data. She doesn't want anyone else to suffer the way she has. Thus, her past personal experience justifies her current behavior, strengthening the story as a whole.

That's not all. It also provides an explanation for why Jo and her husband split up. She couldn't fully commit to their marriage because, due to her past, she's afraid of loss. She pushed her husband away so that she wouldn't be in a position to lose him the way she lost her dad.

Note that Jo's failed marriage isn't extraneous backstory, included to round out Jo's character. It's essential to the film because her estranged husband will join her for the ride!

One more thing: at the end of the second act, a tornado almost kills Jo's Aunt Meg and destroys Meg's home. Critically, this reminds audiences of what is at stake right before the climax, and consequently, recharges their emotional investment in its outcome. Plus, since audiences know that Jo's family was already victim of a tornado, Meg's experience has extra resonance.

You might be thinking that this is all well and good when you're writing a story with lots of action or thrills.

But what if you're writing a romance or a comedy?

Then, it's not so easy. Unless your hero is a firefighter, you probably can't begin your story by putting someone's life at stake.

True, true. But to get audiences to worry, you just need to put *something* at stake. It doesn't have to be someone's life.

For instance, in your opening sequence, you could show your hero at a copy & print shop. Having picked up a staggering stack of thick reports, he desperately navigates through traffic to reach his workplace on time.

It might not be 100% clear what will happen if your hero is late. Still, audiences know that some kind of unwanted consequence will ensue. This, granted, is not as gripping as the opening of *Twister*. But it doesn't have to be. The level of tension it generates is perfectly suited for your genre.

Taking this hypothetical example one step further, let's say that your hero does arrive at work in the nick of time. Whew! He does a little victory dance. (Privately, of course.) He delivers the reports to his boss, who promptly fires him.

Surprise!

Notice that the hero's initial ordeal has added benefits besides generating tension that mildly sucks audiences into your story. It not only creates a minor reversal (audiences would be worried about him being late, not about him getting fired), it also intensifies the impact of the reversal itself.

Because your hero has been dismissed, audiences would be inclined to feel sorry for him. This sympathy, as intended, creates a bond between them and him, heightening their emotional investment in later events. Furthermore, this sympathy will be amplified to some degree since audiences just witnessed your hero's initial trials—and now know that he endured his suffering *in vain*.

This makes the opening stronger. Maybe not by much, but enough to yield a slight advantage. And, as we both know, to stand out in a crowded marketplace, you need all the advantages you can get!

Humanize Antagonists

Because story stakes inspire emotional involvement, if audiences know what your antagonist will lose should he fail in *his* objective, this can, to a certain degree, make them more sympathetic toward him.

In *The Devil Wears Prada*, editor-in-chief Miranda Priestly is the most demanding and unreasonable of bosses. Audiences see her put the heroine through hell—repeatedly. And yet, when the possibility looms that Miranda may be fired, they don't salivate at her comeuppance. Since they know that her dedication to her job has cost her not one—but two—marriages (stakes of sacrifice), they feel sorry for her.

Similarly, in *Harry Potter and the Half-Blood Prince*, audiences know that if Draco doesn't kill Dumbledore, the villain will kill Draco (stakes of demise). Although they certainly don't want the boy to be successful in his mission, Draco's own terror, however, makes it more difficult to hate him for it.

There's no requirement for you to use stakes to make audiences sympathetic toward your antagonist. Bad guys can be bad guys.

At the same time, you don't want your villains and nemeses to be one-note. You want them to come across like real people, not caricatures. Showing audiences what your antagonist should lose (or has already lost) if he fails to achieve his goal, is one way to go about that.

Additionally, using this method makes the relationship between audiences and antagonists less straightforward and more nuanced and complex. This can increase readers' enjoyment of your story.

It can also spectacularly backfire.

Sometimes, audiences appreciate the ambiguity. At other times, they may prefer the comfort of knowing exactly against whom they should direct their animosity.

As a cautionary tale, watch *Law Abiding Citizen*. Initially, the film presents the villain as a hero, someone who brutally lost his family and is trying to seek justice denied to him by the judicial system. It tries to get audiences to root for his success. And at first, through stakes of justice, the film succeeds.

Problems crop up, though, when the villain's circle of carnage starts to encompass individuals who are remotely, if at all, connected to the loss of his family. Like earlier on, he's a vigilante. Only this time, his actions are not so easy to support.

Because the stakes of justice started off so strong, some audience members will continue to root for the villain till the very end. Others will disengage from him, but unfortunately, due to the way the hero (an ambitious district attorney) is portrayed, they won't fully invest in the hero either.

In the end, the hero "wins," and the villain dies. This outcome infuriates audience members who are still onboard with the villain. Those who disengage from the villain won't be that enthused either. They can't be, not when they feel so lukewarm toward the hero.

At the end of the day, the film provides an uneven, and ultimately dissatisfying, experience for both groups (which, incidentally, is further aggravated by a huge credibility issue).

One more point before we move on: you can also apply this technique to your hero. If you want to get audiences to support morally questionable behavior (sometimes the very kind that villains typically engage in), then make sure to emphasize what's at stake should your hero fail.

In *Avatar*, for example, Jake infiltrates the heroine's world under false pretenses. The duplicity, nevertheless, isn't alienating because his motives are so compelling. If he wins the trust of the Na'vi tribe, he'll regain his legs—and his freedom.

In *Gone in 60 Seconds* (2000), Memphis Raines has to steal 50 cars in one night. Auto theft isn't exactly behavior that the average movie-goer would rally behind. But they enjoy the high-octane ride without reservation since they know stealing the cars is the only way Memphis can prevent his little brother from getting killed by a crime boss (stakes of demise).

History provides us with another great example. If Henry VIII maltreated and murdered his wives to procure a male heir in order to prevent civil war from erupting in England after his death (stakes of general protection), then his actions will be easier to sympathize with. In the hands of a skilled writer like Mario Puzo (and a skilled director like Francis Ford Coppola), audiences—as they do while watching *The Godfather*—might even root for Henry to commit murder.

If, on the other hand, Henry's motivation to produce a male heir, and hence, eliminate the wives who couldn't fulfill his objectives, solely arose through his notions of legacy (stakes of reputation), his behavior is almost impossible to support.

Almost.

Again, a talented writer might be able to successfully sell audiences on the idea. Perhaps, you too, are up for the challenge!

Enhance Pacing

Remember when we discussed strategies to remind audiences about the stakes? I recommended that you use reminders in order to maintain the emotional bond between audiences and the stakes.

Reminders have another benefit: they provide a change in pace.

To illustrate, let's return to *The Two Towers* and the climactic Battle of Helm's Deep. Cutting away to the stakes, as we already covered, is a powerful way to remind audiences what the battle is all about. As a bonus, it also gives audiences respite from the action.

If audiences spent all their time on the battlegrounds, the action they witness will start to lose its effect. They will become numb to it, developing action fatigue. In contrast to the battle scenes, the scenes with the stakes are slower in pace; calm and action-free. Although brief, they give audiences enough time to recharge.

So, when the story returns to the battlefield, audiences not only become more emotionally invested in the outcome of the battle, they are also better able to appreciate the action stunts unfolding on-screen.

Likewise, in *The Perfect Storm*, the mini-subplot with Bobby's girlfriend doesn't just add an extra layer of poignancy to the ending.

It also brings the story back to land, occasionally providing relief from the monotony of the stormy ocean. This change in scenery enables audiences to better enjoy the Atlantic action when the story, once again, leaves land for water.

As ever, you have to assess how your choices affect momentum. Oftentimes, the tradeoff will be worth it. By taking the time to remind audiences about the stakes, your story momentum might dissipate a little, but the benefits (increased emotional resonance, a change in pace) more than make up for it.

Create Suspects and Red Herrings

Even when your victim is a rich guy, it'd be boring for your readers if every suspect were motivated by greed. Reflecting on story stakes can help you avoid such tedium.

Gosford Park is a prime example. Three attempts are made on aristocrat William McCordle's life, each one fueled by a different kind of story stake (noted in italics). Anthony Meredith, an in-law through marriage, can't afford for McCordle to pull out of their business deal. Meredith tries (but fails) to kill McCordle to ensure his own *livelihood*.

McCordle has a history of seducing his factory workers, and then, when they become pregnant, forcing them to give up their babies for adoption. Now grown, one of these children stabs McCordle to exact *justice*. However, this suspect, Robert, merely manages to stab a corpse. McCordle is already dead.

He has been poisoned by his housekeeper, Robert's mother, who unbeknownst to Robert, is still alive. With a servant's gift of anticipation, she knew what Robert planned to do, and executed the task herself to stave off Robert's *demise*. Now, he can never be convicted of murder and sent to the gallows. Now, he is safe.

You can also use story stakes to develop a different kind of red herring. Instead of asking yourself, "What would motivate a suspect to kill the victim?" ask yourself, "What would motivate a suspect *to lie* about it?"

For example, one of the suspects could be an inveterate gambler who promised his wife to quit gambling. On the night of the murder, he was lured back to the blackjack tables. If he tells the police the truth about where he was, he'd have an ironclad alibi—but it would cost him his marriage (stakes of happiness), maybe even custody of his children (stakes of access).

Because of his lies and the activities he engages in to keep the lies going, the gambler will appear suspicious to both police and audiences, even if he doesn't have a motive for murder. Alternately, he could very well have good motive to murder the victim, but he's so confident the police won't dig it up, that he continues to lie about his alibi in order to preserve his family.

Even so, you won't be able to use the gambler as a red herring forever. Once the police poke holes in the false alibi or uncover a possible motive (as they always do!), and arrive on the gambler's doorstep with a warrant for his arrest, stakes of freedom are going to take precedent. The gambler will have to come clean.

Hopefully, at this point, you have another red herring to keep readers guessing, or, alternatively, are ready to reveal the true culprit.

Advance the Plot Without Sacrificing Your Characters

In some stories, your protagonist may be reluctant to engage in a certain activity. At first, this may suit your purposes very well. You need to cover more ground before you get to that point.

But eventually, it will become necessary for that action to happen. You don't want to delay it any longer; you want it to take center stage.

You need to take your story to the very place your protagonist has spent half of it trying to avoid. And you're tempted to have him, apropos of nothing, change his mind. So, so tempted.

Don't do it.

Readers have spent pages and pages with this character. Sometimes, they may even know his mind better than you do!

Once they detect the inconsistency—and don't kid yourself, they will—they will feel that you've betrayed not only your protagonist but also their trust.

Crying out in frustration (and, possibly, contempt), they will put down your story.

This, clearly, is not a recipe for success.

You can't sacrifice a character for the sake of your plot. It will only bring you, and your readers, heartache. You also can't let your plot come to a complete and utter standstill.

So, what should you do?

The solution is simple. Put another stake in play.

That way, your protagonist won't be servicing the plot at the expense of his character. Instead, he'll be *servicing the stakes*, and readers can easily buy into his change of heart.

They'll understand that circumstances change. They'll readily accept that he has no choice but to go against his principles, personality, or penchant for lurking at the periphery of all the action.

You've already seen one example of this in chapter 4, when we discussed the "Honor Among Thieves" episode of *White Collar*. As a quick refresher, because the stakes were raised, Neal can participate in the artwork heist, thereby backtracking on his earlier decision not to betray Peter, without incurring complaints of contrivance from audiences.

Here's another example, also heist-themed, from *The Usual Suspects*. Keyser Soze, a criminal mastermind, wants a band of small-time crooks to participate in a cocaine heist worth millions. Keaton, one of the crooks, repeatedly resists the overtures made by Soze's emissary.

For one thing, Keaton thinks it's a suicide mission. In his estimation, the risks aren't worth the rewards. For another, Keaton has good reason to distrust both Soze and Soze's emissary. Finally, Keaton is also trying to make an honest living for the sake of his girlfriend, a clean-cut attorney.

Keaton's resistance serves the plot very well…until it comes time for the heist to actually occur. To advance the story, Keaton must agree to participate. But if he changes his mind all of a sudden, the movie's credibility would be shot to shreds. Even with the surprise twist ending, the film would not continue to enjoy the rave reviews it does.

So how did screenwriter Christopher McQuarrie make Keaton's change of heart believable and not contrived?

He upped the stakes. Keaton learns that his girlfriend will be killed unless he participates. Faced with these new stakes of demise, Keaton, quite credibly, caves. Qualms notwithstanding, he has no choice but to do his best to successfully pull off the heist.

With Keaton's cooperation secured, the climax (including its twist ending) can proceed on schedule, and audiences eat it all up with a spoon the size of an ice cream scoop.

A Few Good Men advances its story forward using the same technique, but links the stakes to a character other than the hero. If Dawson pleads guilty to involuntary manslaughter, Kaffee can have Dawson (and his co-defendant) home in 6 months. Logically, Dawson should take the deal. Six months in jail, as Kaffee puts it, "is nothing. It's a hockey season." But Dawson can't accept.

Why not?

To have a courtroom climax, the case has to go to trial. It can't be stalled with a plea bargain. The story will be cut short before it ever really has a chance to begin.

This reason works for the writer. Unfortunately, it doesn't work for audiences, who need something more.

Screenwriter Aaron Sorkin gave them more. He put another stake in play. Or more accurately, he pitted one stake against another.

For Dawson, an admission of guilt would mean that he had behaved dishonorably—and honor is the cornerstone of his personal code of conduct. Thus, he can't plead guilty. Not because the story requires his refusal in order to continue, but because he values stakes of reputation over stakes of freedom.

Having been sold on the idea, audiences can, without complaint, accept Dawson's decision.

Hence, they get a gripping finale. Kaffee gets his opportunity for growth. The film gets an Oscar nod for Best Picture.

Everybody wins!

- chapter ten -

MAKING REAL MAGIC

Magic tricks are fun to think about.

In terms of being a successful screenwriter or author, magic tricks typically boil down to networking and marketing.

Networking with Hollywood assistants and utilizing the latest savvy book-marketing technique can definitely yield results. However, they're usually short-term solutions.

They get your foot in the door. They get somebody to read the first page of your screenplay or novel.

But, to achieve your dreams, you need more than that.

You need readers who go *all* the way.

You need a studio executive to keep on reading till page 110, and become so impressed with your screenwriting talent, he calls his assistant to schedule a meeting with you.

You need a bookworm to keep on reading till page 350, and become so enthralled with your novel, she tells all her friends to buy your book (and its sequel).

For long-term success, you need *real* magic.

And that is what stakes provide.

Building a network and trading in some favors with a hotshot producer's assistant won't get him to rave about your script to his boss.

Revamping your ebook cover or engaging in a 99 cent promotion won't make a fiction junkie stay up all night to finish your novel.

Stakes, on the other hand, can do both.

They are your long-term strategy for epic sales. They're what great storytelling careers are built on.

Investing the time to master story stakes now should pay off in the future, and accelerate your entry into the big leagues. It is my sincere wish that the knowledge you gained from this book will help you get there.

May your writing career be long, illustrious, and filled with real magic.

༃

FINISH THAT DRAFT*
TODAY.

*and make it awesome!

When you've mastered story structure, you'll write better stories—faster.

Interested? Here's how it works:

With story structure, you have markers to write toward.

You don't have to spend your (limited) writing time wondering where to take your story...or asking yourself, *What happens next?*

You'll know.

Plus, you won't have to build structure into your screenplay or novel after the fact. This should reduce your revision time. Significantly.

In a nutshell, you save time AS you write and AFTER you write. Cool, right?

Wait, 'cause it gets better.

Story structure generates the up-and-down rhythm—the roller-coaster ride—that keeps audiences engaged from beginning to end of your story.

SMARTER STORY STRUCTURE

Get on audiences' good side
Give them a roller-coaster ride

With my online course, Smarter Story Structure, you'll learn practical tips for overcoming plot problems that audiences often gripe about. Things like:

- the story starts too slowly (according to a Goodreads survey, 46.4% of readers abandon novels for this reason)
- the story doesn't get going until halfway through (this happened in almost a quarter of scripts read by a studio reader in a year)
- the middle "runs out of gas" (even John Grisham admits this is a tricky issue)
- the climax doesn't deliver fireworks, merely sparklers
- the story is the right length...but isn't a good read (uh-oh)

Because this multimedia course is online, you can take it from the comfort and convenience of your own home.

It'll be like getting all the great takeaways from a weekend writing seminar... without dealing with bad traffic, hotel fare, and airport lines.

So what are you waiting for? Enroll now!

HTTP://SCRIBEMEETSWORLD.COM/3AS/

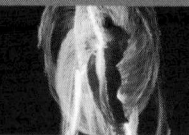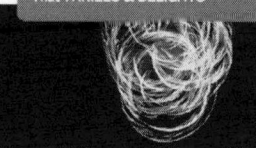

Printed in Great Britain
by Amazon